walking
the steps of
CINCINNATI

walking
the steps of
CINCINNATI

A Guide to the Queen City's Scenic & Historic Secrets

Mary Anna DuSablon

Second Edition, Revised and Updated by
Connie J. Harrell & John Cicmanec

Maps by Brian E. Balsley

ohio university press

athens

Ohio University Press, Athens, Ohio 45701
ohioswallow.com
© 2014 by Ohio University Press
© 1998 by Mary Anna DuSablon

To obtain permission to quote, reprint, or otherwise reproduce or
distribute material from Ohio University Press publications, please
contact our rights and permissions department at
(740) 593-1154 or (740) 593-4536 (fax).

Printed in the United States of America
Ohio University Press books are printed on acid-free paper ♾™

24 23 22 21 20 19 18 17 16 15 14   5 4 3 2

Books by Mary Anna DuSablon published by Ohio University Press:
Cincinnati Recipe Treasury: The Queen City's Culinary Heritage
America's Collectible Cookbooks: The History, the Politics, the Recipes

All photographs courtesy of Connie J. Harrell and John Cicmanec
Book design by Chiquita Babb

Library of Congress Cataloging-in-Publication Data
DuSablon, Mary Anna, 1939–2005.
  Walking the steps of Cincinnati / Mary Anna DuSablon. — Second
edition / revised and updated by Connie J. Harrell & John Cicmanec ;
maps by Brian Edward Balsley.
    pages cm
  Includes bibliographical references and index.
  ISBN 978-0-8214-2081-2 (pb : alk. paper) — ISBN 978-0-8214-4479-5 (pdf)
  1. Cincinnati (Ohio)—Tours. 2. Walking—Ohio—Cincinnati—
Guidebooks. 3. Staircases—Ohio—Cincinnati—Guidebooks. I. Harrell,
Connie J. II. Cicmanec, John. III. Title.
  F499.C53D87 2014
  977.1'78—dc23
                        2014000857

*To the generous and caring Cincinnatians—public servants
and private citizens—who help keep the public
stairways and sidewalks clean, safe,
maintained, and architecturally beautiful*

*To those who hang the step signs and street signs,
paint the crosswalks, and plant flowers along the way
I hope this guidebook brings you well-deserved satisfaction.*

contents

The Legendary Staircases

Mount Adams

Mount Auburn

Price's Hills

Mount Tusculum

The Western Terraces

Twelve Memorable Stepways

foreword

THE FIRST EDITION of Mary Anna's guide invited readers to experience Cincinnati's historical neighborhoods in a way unique to the city: through urban hikes built around the sets of steps that dot the City of Seven Hills. The book gives the hikes context by including the history and development of each neighborhood and how those communities contributed to the growth of the city as a whole.

This new version of her book reflects the changing condition of the steps and guides hikers around derelict or closed steps, while maintaining Mary Anna's vision for each hike.

Mary Anna DuSablon has left all of us a legacy of appreciation for the beauty and history within our city. Whether your hike takes you through one of our distinct neighborhoods or provides a vista point for the majestic Ohio River, or does both, you will be treated to a historical adventure as well as an exhilarating workout. In Cincinnati, an invigorating and enriching experience is just around the corner.

Roxanne Qualls
Mayor, City of Cincinnati, 1993–99

preface to the 2014 edition

In 2009, I discovered Mary Anna DuSablon's *Walking the Steps of Cincinnati*. I began walking the tours of Fairmount, the neighborhood of my childhood. Then, because each walking tour proved to be a living history lesson about the people and events in its neighborhood, I wanted to walk every tour; I wanted to learn more about Cincinnati's history. Buildings, steps, and sidewalks that previously had passed by unnoticed in a car suddenly took on significance.

Following a walking tour is like being a tourist in a foreign city: There's so much to see and so much to learn. I had always lived on the West side of Cincinnati, in several of its neighborhoods. Suddenly I was discovering the East side and its beautiful neighborhoods. On one of my East-side walks, I stopped to chat with a woman working on the flowerbed in her front yard. This woman, a retired Cincinnati librarian and co-worker of the book's author, told me that Mary Anna had died of cancer.

Because of her death, John Cicmanec and I decided to take on the task of updating the changes that have occurred to all 35 walks from the original 1997 edition of *Walking the Steps of Cincinnati*. We have changed the path of each walk to use existing sidewalks and streets. However, the background and historical descriptions of the first edition have remained intact, as written by Mary Anna.

John and I have maintained both the content and format of the original edition, deleting walking routes that no longer exist. One walk, Walk 33, Cincinnati Skywalk, was eliminated completely because the downtown overhead walkways were taken down several years ago. We wanted the walker to enjoy these walks and to feel safe when doing so. We felt that, in removing steps that are closed, in bad repair, and/or too hazardous to traverse, we were able to bring life back to Mary Anna's walks.

We approached our task in three ways:

1. Where steps are closed, we changed the routing to reconnect to the existing route. For example, in Walk 16, O'Bryonville to the Ohio River (originally the O'Bryonville Social Circles), the Collins Street Steps are now private property and not open to the public. We routed the walker past those steps to continue via Taft to Torrence, Torrence to Elmhurst, picking up the original route at the Elmhurst Steps.

2. Some walks had to be revised due to changes in neighborhoods or the condition of the steps. For example, in Walk 10, Shooter's Hill, the Adler Street Steps between Waverly and

Tremont Streets in South Fairmont, although recently restored, are now overgrown with vegetation, making them impossible to walk. The Merrill Street Steps in Walk 11, North Fairmount, once provided a shortcut to Baltimore Avenue for residents of English Woods. Since the homes of English Woods have been demolished, those steps are now closed. In both walks, we removed undesirable steps without compromising the interest of the walk. On the other hand, with the opening of the new Horseshoe casino, Cincinnati has restored the Liberty Hill Steps that connect Reading Road (near the entrance to the casino) to Mount Auburn. Walks 5, Prospect Hill, and 26, Chris O'Malley, have been rewritten to include these new steps.

3. Since the publication of the original edition, some streets, steps, and landmarks have been renamed. In Walk 2, Garden of Eden, Eastern Avenue has been renamed Riverside Drive. In Walk 7, Mount Hope, the Denver Avenue Steps have two changes: Denver Avenue has been renamed Neff Road; and, during a recent upgrade, the "Public Step Brothers" trademark and date inside a star have been removed. As we walked these routes, John and I met and talked with people living along the way. A young man washing his car outside on Neff Road never knew that, at one time, the street had been called Denver Avenue. On the other hand, a young man we met elsewhere told us his father had been born and raised on Denver Avenue; this man did not know that the street name had changed.

All of the remaining 34 walks have been modified to bring them up to date. John and I enjoyed discovering Cincinnati neighborhoods via the numerous stairways. Whenever we encountered a roadblock, such as closed steps, the help of a local resident got us back on track. Through these encounters we learned why certain steps had been closed to the public. Some folks, once we explained our task, were eager to share their own stories of how the steps impacted their lives.

I think the steps are as much a part of Cincinnati heritage as sausage and beer. Fun for everyone!

Connie J. Harrell

Cincinnati is unique because of its hills. Streets go up and down and around the hills. In the original edition of *Walking the Steps of Cincinnati*, Mary Anna DuSablon described the migration of Cincinnati residents from the flat plain downtown to the surrounding hills. In the second half of the nineteenth century, developers built inclines to transport people up to the top of hills; these inclines were then used daily by the general populace. At a time before cars, when people traveled by foot, the shortest, most direct route was desired. Because streets were limited in grade and climbed a hill gradually following a roundabout route, often with switchbacks, staircases containing 100–300 risers provided a convenient, direct connection from the bottom of a hill to the top. Instead of walking 15 minutes for one mile on streets that climbed a hill, a person could travel in three minutes up 225 steps to the same point. For example, in Walk 7, Mount Hope, the Warsaw Avenue Steps provided a direct connection from the lower Price Hill community, containing an elementary school, churches, and restaurants, to the upper Price Hill bedroom community of individual houses. Thirteen years after Mary Anna DuSablon penned the first edition, the Warsaw Avenue Steps have closed. But an adjoining staircase two blocks south, the Staebler Street Steps, are in good repair and in heavy use, still connecting lower and upper Price Hill.

Let the foregoing suffice as an argument for the importance of this book, which serves to connect the past with the present. The historical events described in the text are the past; the walkers viewing the steps and streets of each of the walks are the present. This book serves to educate new generations of their heritage.

This book allows more than a history. By taking the reader off the page, out of his mind's imagination, and onto a real sightseeing tour, it is a hands-on laboratory of history.

John Cicmanec

preface to the first edition

ACCORDING TO THE 1997 Hillside Step update (based on the 1980 City Hillside Stair Study), there are more than 400 sets of steps in Cincinnati, containing more than 16,000 eight-inch (on average) risers. If these public steps were stacked, the vertical ascent would equal about 10,600 feet—two miles straight up. Add in the Hamilton County park stairs and it would be like climbing Clingman's Dome in the Smoky Mountains, twice. Total in the footage of private steps in Cincinnati, residential and otherwise, and who knows? There might be enough steps to reach the moon!

Where did the steps come from and why does Cincinnati have so many? A casual study of Cincinnati's topography from hilltop parks or the Carew Tower's observation deck reveals that hills, ridges, and valleys surround the Basin in a semi-circular fashion, and Cincinnati seems to belong more to Kentucky than Ohio. Because of that, most people eagerly—and erroneously—conclude that Cincinnati is known as a City of Hills, namely Seven. But the facts come from geologists, who explain that Cincinnati is really a City of Valleys; valleys carved in a rolling plain formed more than two million years ago. This "indented edge" of the midwest plains, higher than the Basin, is the crest of an upward fold in the rock called the Cincinnati Arch. Furthermore, scientists continue, the hills number far more than seven.

A century ago, when the Basin had become densely populated and polluted, the citizenry took to the hills by way of the valleys. Settled by different groups of men and women, the hillside and hilltop villages were isolated from one another, developing diverse identities that remain somewhat true even today. Footpaths were steep, treacherous, and often wet, muddy, slick, and eroding. (They still are.) During the 1800s, private citizens erected wooden steps along the steepest footpaths. Many of these original step sites were rebuilt and replaced time and again to the present steps we see today. Some of these stairs, such as those contained in the Overlook Avenue, Norwood, Mount Echo, and Columbia–Tusculum walks, surmounted sites used by Native Americans to observe the white settlers.

Toward the end of the 1800s, as various modes of transportation evolved, trolley car routes starting out in the Basin terminated at the steps, and eventually, at one of the five inclined-plane railways as well. More stairways branched out from the inclines to accommodate residents on the streets underneath. Some of the steps bore names in their own right, for example the Fawn Alley Steps in Mount Lookout and the Hiram Street Steps in Mount Auburn, but most were named after streets for which they were extensions, such as Baymiller, Freeman, and Main. Given such efficient public transportation and excellent public thoroughfares, Cincinnatians did not readily take to the automobile at the turn of the twentieth century as did other cities' dwellers. Between 1939 and 1943, New Deal funds financed hundreds of additional stone and concrete park steps (more on this in the Mount Echo walk).

Throughout the twentieth century, the city maintained the steps, but, unfortunately, the city did not keep records of individual stair history and development until very recently. Today, inspectors date the precast, solid and "hollow," steps as being 1950 or earlier; concrete steps cast-in-place are the most recently built. There are exceptions to this rule. Some steps, such as the Saint Clair Heights Park Steps in Fairmount, are in such hard-to-get places that they were, and will probably always be, precast. The last remaining original wooden steps, the Hiawatha Avenue Steps, also in Fairmount, were replaced by concrete in the 1980s.

In addition to the public steps that you may climb using this guidebook, you may observe thousands of steps leading to private homes, made of the same materials found in the public steps as well as brownstone, limestone, sandstone, brick, tiles, all types of wood, railroad cross-ties, granite, and even cast iron in Mount Auburn. These narrow and wide, steep and spacious steps may be carpeted, painted, or AstroTurfed. They may be inserted in the center of a steep driveway, low enough for the family car to overtake. They may separate the front yard from the back yard, or the patio from the porch. Not too long ago, many riverside homeowners hauled coal in bushel baskets up one, two, three, four, and five lengthy flights of steps, and they still shoulder groceries in this same taxing manner. Steps lend themselves to excellent landscaping possibilities, and the owners of many stepped homes on these routes could qualify for national honors if such a thing existed.

Cincinnati has another topographical distinction. Nicknamed "Landslide City, U.S.A." by national geologists and surveyors, it is the most landslide prone area in the country based on damage done per capita. Landslide damage in Hamilton County between 1973 and 1978 was $31 million, or $5.80 per capita per year. The Cincinnati steps did not escape harm during this period, nor have they since. The wear and tear of daily usage takes its toll, and step maintenance costs, including overgrowth and trash removal, can run in the tens of thousands per job. Nevertheless, the Cincinnati steps are an integral part of our city's infrastructure. This singularly distinct, priceless heritage helps set Cincinnati apart from other cities as a truly unique place to live and an adventurous destination for visitors. The steps offer tantalizing, stunning, and breathtaking views. They offer exercise. They link communities in a pedestrian-friendly manner. They show off Cincinnati's history in an attractive, accurate way. Only San Francisco has more public steps than Cincinnati.

There is no doubt that the steps are used. They still serve their original purpose as a convenient means for residents getting from one place to another, particularly for shopping and commuting to and from work. Schoolchildren use them. Runners and walkers use them; teams muscle up and down in training; even parents with babies aboard slick, functional baby carriages manage the steps. Mountain bikes rule. Tourists discover them and can't believe we take them for granted. Children stage many an exciting drama on the steps. Dogs adore them. Lovers woo and laugh and tease and talk and argue on the stairways. Workers take their lunch. Penitents pray. Children ride the banisters; one of the ways city inspectors decide which steps are being used is by how shiny the banisters are.

What made me decide to write about the Cincinnati steps? Although I walk every day, it became apparent to me that my knees needed more activity, such as stepclimbing. I fondly recalled the steps of my youth—those in the East End, Mount Lookout, Eden Park, O'Bryonville and Walnut Hills—and I began revisiting those good old days. Much to my surprise, the staircases were even lovelier than I remembered. As I walked, I yearned to show people what a satisfying workout I'd worked out (my reputation as an insufferable Cincinnati ambassador was already well known to friends and colleagues), and the most logical thing to do, it seemed, was write a book. Without any idea of what I was getting into, I improvised two walks in Mount Adams by simply asking people where the steps were. Most people I talked to only knew about the steps in their own community. Finally, I got the bright idea of contacting the city. At the first meeting between myself and engineers Jim Mills, Mark Ginty, and Willie Gay, the conversation went something like this:

Me: "I've already designed a couple of great walks around Mount Adams. Can you give me topographical maps for the places where the other steps are located?"

Them: "Well, uh, yes, but there are hundreds of them."

Me, excitedly: "Oh, I know, I know! There must be two hundred steps leading up to Immaculata from Martin Street alone."

Them, patiently: "No . . . you don't understand. There are hundreds of *sets* of steps."

My ancestors the Frawleys, living in Hamilton County in the early 1800s, bought land from and sold land to Nicholas Longworth the elder. The Koehlers and Linnemanns helped settle California, Ohio, as proprietors of the general store and post office. Great-Grandpa George Linnemann was a one-term city councilman; Great-Uncle

Henry founded a funeral business in Covington. Grandpa Tom Maxwell came to Cincinnati from New York to help build the Water Works pumping station in California and stayed to work on several other Water Works projects, the Ault Park pavilion, and various roads, bridges, viaducts—and steps. Aunt Therese played saxophone for bands that played at Ault Park in the 1920s. Uncle "Dutch" (Edgar George) is considered the Mayor of Columbia–Tusculum. My father, Charles Martin, was the city's Chief of Homicide from 1956 to 1962. Mom and her sisters were election judges and PTA officers. Growing up, I rode the Mount Adams Incline and visited the Rookwood Pottery. I improvised trolley and bus transfer routes that occasionally left me at the end of the line, at the end of the day, with no alternative but to walk home or call my frustrated father. When I got a job as a stenographer-typist at City Hall, the Building Code kept me from being bored out of my wits. To get to the point here, my ancestry and life experience made me feel that the City of Cincinnati was there to explore and experience—and I did just that.

During the three years of research undertaken for this book, visiting each step site five to ten times because I am a stickler for detail, my bichon-poo Big Ben and I were never once threatened with harm from humans. We saw a couple of drug deals. And Ben was once attacked by a retriever-chow who meant to protect his mistresses' children, but let me tell you, we wrestled that cur to the ground. Ben and I did experience some nasty weather. We took shelter under the Elmhurst (some call it Torrence) Avenue Bridge from hail the size of marbles. The 8th Street bridge protected us from lightning. We sat out tornado sirens in an Alms Park ravine. We forged ahead against wind that did not want us to succeed; through cold, hard rain and warm, balmy rain; through snow and ice. In winter, Ben coated his feet with salt and dreadful chemicals. I forgot my water bottle on a most humid 100-degree day and nearly collapsed. We were standing on Mount Echo's summit on a cloudy April 1997 day when it became perfectly obvious the black, boiling Ohio River would flood. We drove through the flash flood in Newtown.

In addition to communications of every sort with various historical society members, I attended community meetings in South Fairmount and North Fairmount where the opening of the Saint Clair Heights Park Steps, after ten years closed, was the hot item on the agenda. The argument was familiar: Higher-ups hoping to prevent lower-downs from regaining access to the park facilities—their own heritage! "The steps will become avenues of crime!" was the rallying cry. Immediately, two arguments come to mind when I hear this. The first is that crime in the neighborhood of the convenience store doesn't result in its closing. Second, the image of sweaty, breathless robbers running up and down the steps, burdened with VCRs and bicycles and silverware, is downright funny.

Because of these shallow arguments, and because those of us who cherish these precious landmarks haven't done enough to see that our heritage isn't further spoiled, many picturesque staircases have already vanished. Fewer than 300 staircases are in tip-top shape; some are virtually closed. Yet, crime and antisocial behavior lessens where people and pets stroll on a regular basis, where lighting is installed and woodsy areas are kept clean, where repairs to the infrastructure are regularly carried out, and where responsible residents act as observation tools for the police department.

I can't begin to express how grateful I am that I had the chance to freely roam this beautiful, cosmopolitan, and satisfying 200-year-old city. How much fun it was inventing these walks and refining them, exploring—like an anthropologist—wonder-full neighborhoods, intriguing thoroughfares, and secret passageways. Ben and I met some of the kindest, most interesting people in the world on the Cincinnati steps. We ran into old friends. We helped rescue a stray dog and thus earned a beer at the Main Street Blues Cafe. We found a five-dollar bill on the ground near a bus stop. We studied our notes in comfy coffee cafes. We reveled in the real (not recorded) church bells we heard. We accumulated first-rate memories and riveting stories.

My knees quit hurting and I lost five pounds. I felt such exhilaration. I hope others will feel the same.

Acknowledgments

Gillian Berchowitz, David Sanders, Chiquita Babb, and the staff of the Ohio University Press; and Julia Marcel DuSablon, editor—all superb teammates.

City of Cincinnati: Willie Gay, Jim Mills, Mark Ginty, and Rich Szekeresh, Public Works Engineers—without whose cooperation the project would have taken five years instead of three. Bill Lindsay, Signage; Michael Moore, Architect; Dave Rupe, Crosswalks; Michelle Burns, Recreation Department; Paul Tonis, Park Board; and Vivian Wagner, Bettman Library Archivist. Rebecca Lynn Martin, Cincinnati Police Mountain Bike Patrol (and my niece).

Public Library of Cincinnati: Many thanks, as always, to the professional staff in the Newspaper and Census Archives, and in the History Department, and in the Rare Book Archive.

University of Cincinnati: Kevin Grace, Blegen Library Archivist and good friend; Dr. Michael Sitko, Physics Department; Kaes Dejong, Geology Department; and Christos Damakas and Jennifer Wallace, Alumni Association.

Price Hill Historical Society: Many thanks to Valda Moore, Executive Secretary; and Andy Stryker for walking and critiquing the Price Hill walks.

Norwood: Rick Dettmer, Development Director; and Mike Fraley, Engineering Department. Newport: Christopher Novak, Director of Community Services.

Ernie B. Smith, for walking and critiquing the Fairmount walks; and Lois Broerman of the North Fairmount Community Center.

Paul and Deborah Anderson, owners of the Anderson Ferry; Charles DuSablon of Playhouse in the Park; Gary Hillebrand of Price Hill, and his dog Murphy; Michael Hurt, Juvenile Historian, Price Hill; Kathleen Schuermann, former Mount Adams resident; Len Thomas of Botanics; and Victoria Warman of Norwood. Jeanmarie DuSablon for the San Francisco step book. Theresa Rose King for her encouragement; Joseph Beaver.

S. T. Bailey, who says I can thank him later.

And particularly to the thousands of people I ran into on Cincinnati's steps and streets, whose names I do not know, who helped me piece together the walks and verify the history.

introduction

WALKING THE STEPS OF CINCINNATI is a field guide to 34 ultra-scenic, "perpendicular public paths" throughout twenty-six distinctive neighborhoods. The primary 22 walks contain staircases that are legendary for one reason or many reasons, including length and local prominence. The 12 additional walks are more or less irresistible, depending on your affection for the neighborhood or stepways in general. Cincinnatians are familiar with the most famous flights of steps, best known by the street names for which they serve as extensions. Other stairs promise the thrill of discovery.

Each walk in "The Legendary Staircases" is described by length, the character of the neighborhood and the realm of its vistas, how many stairs there are and how steep they are, and so on. Precise, easy-to-follow directions for your circumambulation follow, with a neighborhood map. Historical essays offer a glimpse into each area's singular cultural heritage.

The "Twelve Memorable Stepways" are briefly outlined for your extended enjoyment. Directions to the starting points are not given for the simple reason that they are for the most part well known and can be quickly ascertained on any city map. Most readers will approach the various walks by car. Downtown residents and hotel guests may access the Mount Adams, Mount Auburn, Fairview, Over-the-Rhine, and Ohio River walks by foot. All starting points are on Metro routes.

Depending on how fast you walk and how long you linger at the fantastic sights, each walk takes a minimum of 45 minutes. Rest, water, refreshments, and toilet facilities are usually close by, although some park facilities, including pumps to give your dog a drink of water, are seasonal.

City and park benches can usually be found by the foot-weary, and there are always the steps themselves when a respite is needed. Many of the steps are illuminated at night, all night. Most of the steps are in excellent condition and in reasonably safe, well-traveled neighborhoods, unless otherwise noted.

Not all the Cincinnati steps were included; a List of Hillside Steps is available from Public Works. Some steps were redundant or too isolated, including many expressway overpass steps, or, like the cute little steps around Hyde Park Square, not substantial enough to whip up a walk. And unfortunately, some public and park staircases were ruled out because they were in unsafe or thoroughly unpleasant locations.

It would not be a bad idea to read through each walk before you attempt it so that you have a good idea what you're getting into. Some walks, such as Riverside and Oakley, are far easier to accomplish than, say, Mount Harrison.

See you on the Cincinnati steps!

approximate walk lengths in miles

THE DISTANCES LISTED below include the actual measured map distance, plus an additional 0.1–0.2 miles added to account for elevation change. Walks with two listed distances contain alternate routes that are described in the text and clearly shown on the corresponding map.

Walk 1. The Good Friday Pilgrimage: 1.7 miles
Walk 2. Garden of Eden: 2.6 miles
Walk 3. Genius Loci: 2.5 miles
Walk 4. Science Stroll: 2.3 miles
Walk 5. Prospect Hill: 2.3 miles
Walk 6. The Main Street Steps: 2.4 miles
Walk 7. Mount Hope: 2.2 miles
Walk 8. Mount Echo: 1.6 miles
Walk 9. Mount Harrison: 4.0 (or 5) miles
Walk 10. North Fairmount: 1.7 miles
Walk 11. South Fairmount: 2.0 miles
Walk 12. Findlay Market to Bellevue Hills: 2.2 miles
Walk 13. Fairview Hill: 2.2 miles
Walk 14. Brighton Hill: 1.6 (or 1.5) miles
Walk 15. Celebrity Tour: 4.5 (or 4.4) miles
Walk 16. O'Bryonville to the Ohio River: 3.9 (or 4.0) miles
Walk 17. Mount Lookout Square: 2.6 miles
Walk 18. Around Ault Park: 3.5 miles
Walk 19. Grandin Road: 2.9 miles
Walk 20. Overlook Avenue: 3.7 miles
Walk 21. Columbia–Tusculum: 2.8 miles
Walk 22. Riverside: 3.1 miles
Walk 23. Avondale: 2.5 miles
Walk 24. Old Clifton: 2.8 miles
Walk 25. Linwood: 2.7 miles
Walk 26. Chris O'Malley's Ridge Walk: 3.7 miles
Walk 27. Old Milford: 1 mile (approximate). No mapped walk route is provided.
Walk 28. Norwood: 5.1 miles
Walk 29. Oakley: 1.8 miles
Walk 30. Crossing the Ohio River Bridges: 4.2 miles
Walk 31. Riverside Park: 3.2 miles
Walk 32. Sayler Park: 3.7 miles
Walk 33. University of Cincinnati: 1.8 miles
Walk 34. Westwood: 2.8 (or 4.5) miles

THE

LEGENDARY

STAIRCASES

MOUNT ADAMS

I MOVED FROM Knoxville to Cincinnati not expecting to be
able to continue the types of hikes and walks found in Ten-
nessee. Glancing at an ordinary street map, I took exploratory
walks around my Mount Auburn home, and they were quite sat-
isfactory. Soon I was organizing long walks, climbing steps up
to the heights of Mount Adams, crisscrossing through Mount
Auburn, connecting up to Clifton Heights, descending into Fairview, even across the viaducts to Fairmount. I had connected, by
foot, six of Cincinnati's hills with steps I only guessed were there.
If there was a park at the top of a hill, I said to myself, there's got
to be steps. And there were.

Chris O'Malley

Walk No. 1

1.7 miles

The Good Friday Pilgrimage

THIS FIRST WALK features Cincinnati's most famous set of steps, seven flights that connect Saint Gregory Street with Holy Cross Immaculata Church (formerly known as Immaculate Conception Church). At the summit, you are treated to an exhilarating panorama: a 10-mile stretch of the Ohio River; the vast, picturesque Ohio and Kentucky shorelines; the bridges; and the bird's-eye view of the rooftops and chimney pots of Mount Adams. Hundreds of additional steps are included in the heavenward approach from the river basin to the statue of Mary dominating the skyline. Hundreds more guide you down. Back when it was called Mount Ida, Mount Adams was famous for being part of Nicholas Longworth's Catawba grape vineyards. After the vines withered from disease in the mid-1800s, immigrants bought and developed the land. The mount was renamed after a visit by President John Quincy Adams, an amateur astronomer, who came to dedicate the country's first observatory, built on four acres donated by Longworth (the original observatory and the current observatories are discussed in Walk No. 4). Soon Mount Adams was populated with German Catholics, many of whom used the steps to access riverfront factories. These working-class folks were also responsible for establishing Cincinnati's Good Friday pilgrimage up the stairs, which eventually captivated penitents of all faiths. The tradition proliferated, rain or shine, for almost a century (1860–1960), and, although it continues, the one-day ritual is far less dramatic than it once was. Today's climbers and commuters follow this acclaimed route with, perhaps, a more healthful than religious intent. Proposed changes by the community include

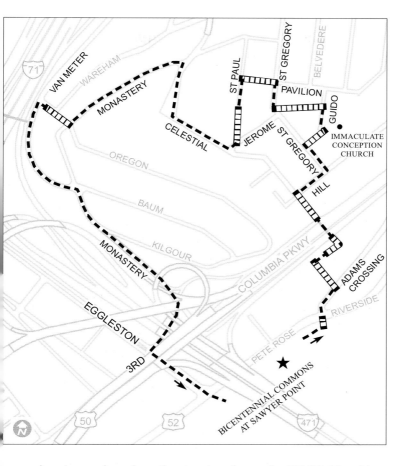

hanging gardens along the steps to enhance the Old World ambiance while protecting one of the city's greatest treasures from erosion and neglect.

Begin at the Bicentennial Commons parking lot at Eggleston Avenue and Pete Rose Way; there is usually a small fee to park.

- Walk east through the parking lot to the **Sawyer Point Steps** that lead up to the merging point of Pete Rose Way, Riverside, and Adams Crossing; or walk east on the Pete Rose Way sidewalk.
- Cross to the sidewalk on the north side of Pete Rose Way, and walk left onto Adams Crossing. Note the old red brick firehouse, elevation 500 feet.
- On the north side of Adams Crossing, walk to the Classical Revival Stone Arch and the first of several sets of the **Celestial Street Steps**. Begin your ascent of these steps.
- Cross the green-railed Celestial Street Bridge over Columbia Parkway and Fort Washington Way—elevation 600 feet. This bridge is a card-carrying member of the National

Historic Register. (Note the additional bridge access steps. As you can see, this walk is easily accessed from 5th Street.)

· At the end of the bridge, go up five more long flights and five short flights to reach the corner of Hill and Celestial Streets, at Riverview Place. Enjoy the view. Turn right.

· Walk one block east to Saint Gregory Street; cross to take in three corner steps; then go left half a block to the final, official, blessed, **Saint Gregory Street Steps**: Seven more flights, 10 to 12 steps each.

· Behold, at the pinnacle, Holy Cross Immaculata Church. Take in the panoramic views. The church promontory is about 800 feet above sea level.

· Follow Guido Street half a block, pausing to read the "Church of the Steps" Mount Adams Preservation Association plaque. Descend the somewhat secluded **Guido Street Steps**, on the left, to Saint Gregory Street.

· Follow Saint Gregory up, half a block, to Pavilion Street and the fountain that designates the more-or-less center of Mount Adams.

· Left on Pavilion Street to climb the tony red-tile-and-cement **Pavilion Street Steps** to Saint Paul Place and the Italian Renaissance–style Holy Cross Monastery and Church, from which emanate the beautiful chimes on the quarter hour. Now privately owned property, this is the site originally occupied by the nation's first observatory; turn left onto Saint Paul Place.

· At the no-outlet end of Saint Paul Place, you will discover the narrow, charming, definitely secluded **Saint Paul Place Steps**. Follow these steps to Jerome Street; turn right.

- Right on Celestial Street; past the Highland Towers; past The Rookwood restaurant. Pause to read the "Mount Adams" Preservation Association plaque.
- When you reach Monastery Street, cross at the crosswalks and begin your steep descent of Monastery Street.
- About halfway down, opposite Oregon Street, take the old-to-sleekly-renovated **Oregon Street Steps** that empty onto the corner of Van Meter Street and Wareham Drive.
- Left on Van Meter Street, curving around a long block to reenter Monastery Street; follow the sidewalks to the bottom.
- Right on 3rd Street. Left on Eggleston Avenue. As you head back to Bicentennial Commons and your parked car, note that the beautifully planted street divider strips contain some of the old cobblestones that used to separate the tangle of railroad tracks (occasionally exposed) in this same location. Eventually, these trains vied for space with automobiles as they carried goods and produce to and from the city's commercial waterfront area. Pause to read the "Little Miami Railroad" City of Cincinnati plaque located on a pillar near the Eggleston–Pete Rose Way crosswalk (more on the railroad is discussed in Walk No. 16).

The Ancient Penitential Drama

Although the Cincinnati Catholic Diocese blessed only the concrete steps fronting Holy Cross Immaculata Church, the fanatically devoted and the younger crowd preferred to hike the scenic surrounding steps up to Mount Adams first. The ritual began at midnight on Holy Thursday and continued for 24 hours, the darkly clad penitents mouthing a silent prayer on each step whether they began on Martin Street, Eggleston Avenue, Court Street, Sycamore Hill, or Saint Gregory Street. Many even prayed on the landings between staircases, accompanying each footstep with an invocation as the queue inched and became denser toward the pinnacle. Heads bowed, eyes averted, conversation was discouraged.

At the top, kneeling on a bench at the base of the large crucifix attached to the outside of the church, the penitent was expected to say a few prayers for the souls departed. Entering the vestibule, a finger-dipped blessing from the marble holy water font was in order. Proceeding down the center aisle, he or she was reminded of the consequences of unrepentant sin by solemn signs of death and damnation. Purple shrouds hid the statues of Mary and the saints from the sinner's imploring glance. The church organ was silent, and in the place of bells, a harsh wooden clacker announced the presence of the priest and acolytes. The salvation of Holy Communion was distributed nearly nonstop, and masses were read on the half-hour. For a small donation, one could light a votive candle—if a fresh wick could be found among the white-hot tiers—to leave behind a plea for forgiveness or hope. Centered within a fog of burning incense, a smaller crucifix reposed on a pillow at the communion rail, where the mourner was expected to crouch and devoutly kiss the five bloody wounds.

Downstairs in the church basement a few pennies bought richly hued or pastel colored holy cards depicting Christ, the Holy Ghost, Mary, or saints favored at the time. Third-class relics, wee scraps of cloth that had touched a cloth that had touched a beatified personage, could be purchased or gazed at in awe. Medals, chains, and rosaries made of silver, gold, crystal, semiprecious stones, colored glass beads, wood, pressed rose petals, and knotted cord were displayed in white gift boxes. For 15 cents you could get a cup of coffee and a breakfast roll, a welcome relief to the morning's fasting.

Leaving Holy Cross Immaculata Church, the penitent continued to Holy Cross Monastery and Church (where the English-speaking, mostly Irish settlers worshipped). As one descended into the catacomb under the church, a copper coffer containing the partial skeleton of a martyr imported from the genuine catacombs of Rome was paid respect. At the grotto of Our Lady of Lourdes, the crutches and braces on exhibition provided an appropriate place for religious ecstasy or for fainting dead away from sheer exhaustion or heatstroke, as some did every year. Here also was a piece of the True Cross, acquired by Father Guido Metassi, the monastery's first abbot, for whom **Guido Street and Steps** were gratefully named.

This was Good Friday in Cincinnati, the commemoration of the torture and crucifixion of Jesus. From the murmur of the early morning Latin Mass, throughout the *miserere* of the most dreadful hours between noon and three o'clock—marking the time Jesus hung on the cross—and until the Holy Saturday wake, the doleful liturgy was observed by the faithful at Holy Cross Immaculata Church as elaborately and sincerely as it was observed at the Vatican in Rome.

Walk No. 2

2.6 miles

Garden of Eden

ALL THE STEPS in this gorgeous, arduous walk are maintained by the Cincinnati Park District and are informally known as the **Eden Park Steps.** They guide you from one thrilling Ohio River outlook to another, through Eden Park's hills and valleys, to Mount Adams, and back again. From the first overlook, Riverside Drive, always involved with river commerce, lies about 300 feet below. Just above Riverside Drive, Columbia Parkway unravels like a shining, curled ribbon paralleling the wide river until both tuck into the domesticated cleavage of the distant eastern hillsides. Across the river, the recently constructed levee belies the fact that before the Markland Dam was built downriver in the 1950s, the white sands of Bellevue's Queen City Beach and Dayton's Sand Bar were highly popular with Kentuckians and Ohioans out for a swim, a rowboat ride, and a day in the sun. Also included in this walk is the Mirror Lake underground reservoir area—where dogs get a chance to stretch their legs and swim, canine style, in the shallow waters of the cap. Ice skating is the sport, for humans, in winter.

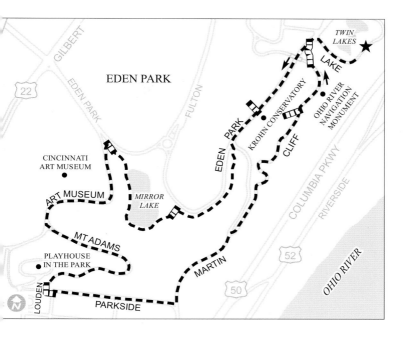

EDEN PARK

TWIN LAKES

LAKE

KROHN CONSERVATORY

OHIO RIVER NAVIGATION MONUMENT

EDEN PARK

CLIFF

CINCINNATI ART MUSEUM

ART MUSEUM

MIRROR LAKE

MT ADAMS

PLAYHOUSE IN THE PARK

COLUMBIA PKWY

RIVERSIDE

MARTIN

52

50

OHIO RIVER

LOUDEN

PARKSIDE

Park at the Eden Park overlook on Lakes Drive, near Twin Lakes, where ducks and waterlilies are occasionally visited by schools of goldfish and remote-control watercraft.

- Exit the park to walk along Eden Park Drive in a westerly direction, passing between the stone eagles and beneath the Melan Arch Bridge, the first steel-reinforced, poured-concrete bridge built in the Midwest. (Steps on the left may be used later at the end of the walk.)
- Continue along Eden Park Drive, or, better yet, follow the path and steps around the front of the Irwin Krohn Conservatory. The outdoor floral display here never ends and is best appreciated on foot.
- Cross Martin Drive, head toward the gazebo, and pick up the paved Frederick Hinkle Floral Trail, named after a man who served on the Park Board for almost 25 years.
- Enter the woods. On your left is the ruin of the partially above-ground Cincinnati reservoir, which has been given over to ballplayers and rock-climbing enthusiasts (Park Board permit needed).
- Follow the trail to a short set of steps on the left. Leave the trail to descend these steps to Mirror Lake Meadow.
- Circle the reservoir, one way or the other, ending up at the hedged Cincinnati Water Works memorial plaque and steps leading up to Art Museum Drive. The elaborately arched gazebo on the edge of the plateau is an old springhouse once

used to access medicinal waters until the spring dried up. (It symbolizes Eden Park on city maps and street signs.)

- Left on Art Museum Drive, curving along the bandstand vale where, since 1872, the refrains of Greek choruses, German oompah bands, 1940s dance bands, the haunting voices of Betty and Rosemary Clooney and other pop singers, folk singers, jazz bands, and rock and rollers have sounded through the trees.
- Pass the Cincinnati Art Museum.
- Enter the *Do Not Enter* end of Mount Adams Circle, which encircles Playhouse in the Park.
- Continue around, taking in the vistas and overlooks, to the conspicuous stone, handrailed stairs on the left. Descend into the northwest corner of Mount Adams, Louden Street, at Parkside Place.

- Follow Parkside to the bottom (Martin Drive), peeking in at the courtyards along the way.
- Left on Martin Drive. Begin your long climb up the twisting hillside, at some point crossing Martin Drive and entering the *Do Not Enter* end of Cliff Drive. You are now on the other side of the reservoir ruin; it was here at the service road where infamous bootlegger George Remus murdered his wife in 1927, after she aided the State's case and moved in with a government agent. Pleading insanity, Remus was hospitalized for five months and then set free. Years later, it is said, the gun was found in the bushes by a child on an Easter egg hunt.
- The red-brick building on your left once housed the Water Works pumping station for Walnut Hills; it later served as a police radio station.
- Finally, you will overtake the Ohio River Navigation monument, a 30-foot high, gray granite obelisk that marks the halfway point of the Ohio River between Pittsburgh, Pennsylvania, and Cairo, Illinois, where it joins the Mississippi River. Pause to read the plaque. President Hoover stood at this site to dedicate the monument. Cannons were placed here during the Civil War, aimed south.
- Continue along Cliff Drive back to the Melan Arch Bridge, where a sturdier staircase with handrail will take you to the same place—the area where you parked your car. (Once you are familiar with this route, reverse it for a different perspective.)

- The newly renovated steps from Cliff Drive down to the Krohn Conservatory introduce another lively walk. Wander around

the conservatory, and then cross Eden Park Drive at the crosswalk to encounter more steps that lead to the Pioneers, Presidents, Authors, and Heroes Groves, another old water tower, this one designed as a castle keep, and the Vietnam War memorial. Step-paths crisscross throughout.

The Longworth Name

When Nicholas Longworth the elder, age 21, arrived from England in 1803, he had to scrimp to pay for his two-dollar-a-week room at a boarding house on Front Street. At his death in 1863, he was one of the richest men in America; only William Astor paid more real estate taxes than did Nicholas Longworth. He made his fortune by buying and selling land, and in the early years, his peers ridiculed him for investing in "swampland," such as Jacob Burnet's cow pasture in Clifton. A few years later, the last laugh was his when he sold it at a million-dollar profit. The acreage that Longworth bought and held onto, however—stretching from Mount Adams where his Catawba grapevines burgeoned throughout what is now Eden Park and into Walnut Hills—he fancied his Garden of Eden. Maps of the time concede the point. He built his mansion, "Rookwood," on Grandin Road (the mansion was razed in 1954).

In 1807, Longworth married widow Susan Howell-Connor on Christmas Eve, in the Basin's first red brick building. They were a

couple united in civic-mindedness; the Longworth name was be-hind nearly every artistic endeavor in the city at the time.

Nicholas and Susan's son Joseph married Annie Rives; the cou-ple endowed the Art Museum and Academy. They had three chil-dren, Nicholas II, Landon, and Maria, known as "Ia." Nicholas II sired Republican congressman Nicholas III, who married Theodore Roosevelt's daughter Alice. Alice, whose mother died in child-birth, was said to be emotionally rejected by her father and later by her husband. She had a nasty reputation in political circles, but Nicholas III was well liked despite flagrant episodes of adultery. The "Longworth" House Office Building in Washington, D.C., bears his name. Dr. Landon Longworth, the second child of Joseph and Annie, died at age 32 years.

The most talented of the three children was the extraordinary Maria Longworth. She was one of the women responsible for insti-tuting the Cincinnati May Festival and establishing the Cincinnati Symphony Orchestra. She was the artist-founder of the internation-ally acclaimed Rookwood Pottery and a fine artist in her own right.

Other family names might be better known to Cincinnatians, but the legacy left by the Longworth family endures with character-istic affection, good humor, and exquisite taste.

Walk No. 3

2.5 miles

Genius Loci

THIS ULTIMATE WALK, full of drama, challenges the hiker with three Mount Adams hillocks. Each stairway is a masterpiece. Im-

pressive landmarks are abundant, and the walk begins and ends at the Cincinnati Art Museum, where you may want to work in a visit. It would be impossible to list the names of the many artists, ceramists, and sculptors who left their footprints on these narrow streets (originally cobblestone flanked by boardwalks) and fanciful flights of stone steps, but they were once traversed by Farny, Duveneck, Longworth and company, and their students—many of whom lived in Mount Adams rather than face the climb on a daily basis. Mount Adams continues to attract artistic, literary, and athletic dwellers, who walk and run the steps for exercise. In addition to the grand views, tradi-

tional boxy homes, rowhouses, and eclectic townhouses and condos, many with petite gardens and quaint windowboxes, can be observed and enjoyed throughout the walk.

Park in the Cincinnati Art Museum parking lot.

- Follow the signs to the parking lot behind the art museum (across from the Main Entrance). Turn left into the parking lot. Locate the metal pole on the right marking the **Art Museum Steps.** Park your car. Return to the steps and ascend to the asphalt path and a series of fieldstone steps that empty onto Eden Park Drive. (These steps once accessed a double-decker bridge with streetcars on the top and pedestrians on the bottom that connected this hill with the rest of Eden Park.)
- Walk west on Eden Park Drive to Gilbert Avenue.
- Walk left (south) on Gilbert Avenue. Continue on Gilbert past the studios of local television station WCPO, Channel 9. Next to WCPO is the formidable rampart that marks the Elsinore Place entrance to Eden Park. In 1883, the Water Works needed a valve house to regulate the flow of water

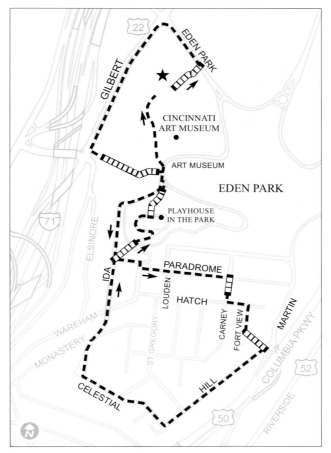

between the reservoir and the Ohio River at the same location in which a gateway was needed for Eden Park. After Charles Hannaford, son of famous Cincinnati architect Samuel Hannaford, saw famous Cincinnati actor James Murdoch in the title role of *Hamlet*, he was inspired to design the valve house to replicate the theatrical set. The tower and street were named Elsinore, after the tower and gate at Hamlet's Castle Kronberg.

- Pass through the arch, aiming straight ahead to the breathtaking fossilized limestone and sandstone **Elsinore Place Steps** leading back up to Mount Adams—otherwise known as "the Hill."
- Top out in one of the mount's few free parking lots; turn right and follow the lot or the sidewalk to Ida Street.
- Left on Paradrome Street, crossing Wareham Drive and Louden Street, and down the hill to Carney Street.
- Right to travel up the **Carney Street Steps** to Hatch Street.
- Left on Hatch Street.

- Right on the block-long, brick-lined Fort View Place, going to the end. It was the establishment of Fort Washington in 1789 that decided where the Ohio River's major city would be situated, and the settlement, now identified by the Western-Southern time and temperature sign, was once visible from the place you are standing. (Downtown, there is a Fort Washington explanatory monument on Ludlow Street at 4th Street.) During the Civil War, several cannons were poised here over the declivity, ready for action but never fired.
- Enter the iron fencing and descend through the steep, wooded crevice via the 150 **Fort View Place Steps** to Hill Street.
- Re-climb Mount Adams via its first paved street—Hill Street—glimpsing memorable views framed between homes until you reach Hill Street's scenic end.
- Right on Celestial Street for about three blocks to the large parking lot at the corner of Celestial and Celestial. Walk south through the parking lot to the cliff edge overlooking the Ohio River. Below on the hillside are the remains of the Mount Adams Incline. Next door, the Highland Towers apartment building is on the site of the former Highland House, which serviced the top of the incline. Return to the corner of Celestial and Celestial, and read the metal plaque of the Mount Adams Preservation Association. Walk west on Celestial.
- Continue around to the art deco, recessed-lighted Ida Street Viaduct; cross the viaduct. (The **Monastery Street Steps** seen here are used in Walk No. 4.)
- Return to the corner of Ida and Paradrome, the neighborhood of best-selling author Stephen Birmingham. Bisecting this corner are steps ascending to the Cincinnati Playhouse in the Park. Climb them, and follow the driveway to the front of the playhouse. There is a circular driveway around the

perimeter of the playhouse. Follow this driveway left (west-ward) of the main entrance.

- As you circle the playhouse, note the views to the south and west of the Ohio River bridges, downtown buildings, and Cincinnati Museum Center. You are at elevation 800 feet above sea level. As you walk behind the building to the north entrance to the playhouse, you will see the top of a staircase going down the north slope. Descend the railed, terraced, and landscaped steps heading toward Art Museum Drive. At the bottom of the steps, cross Art Museum Drive at the crosswalk, and follow the sidewalk back to the museum entrance and your parked car.

Atop the Mount Adams Incline

Transecting the Hill from Loch Street (pronounced Lock; it once paralleled Eggleston Avenue) to Celestial Street, about 945 slant-feet, the Mount Adams Inclined-Plane Railway opened in 1876. It was the fourth incline built in Cincinnati; all four were privately funded. Patterned after the popular Main Street Incline, the Mount Adams Incline had two parallel tracks supported by a heavy wooden trestle and stone retaining walls over Kilgour, Baum, and Oregon Streets. In the beginning, passengers boarded a stationary car permanently mounted on a level, wooden, cable-drawn platform to go up and down; later, the platforms welcomed streetcars at either end. The trolley rode smoothly and directly from its street rails onto the platform rails and off again onto the street rails at the top, and vice versa. The ride took less than five minutes. Running along the "south" side of the Mount Adams Incline, punctuating the wooded hillside from Loch Street to Celestial Street, were four flights of steps; these were added to accommodate the residents of Kilgour, Baum, and Oregon Streets.

On the incline's opening day, stockholders invited special guests to board free of charge the two cars named Nicholas Longworth and Martin Baum; all other riders paid a nickel. For almost 75 years, the incline conveniently brought the Mount Adams residents into the city to work, to shop, to worship, to play, and home again. It also served the students, teachers, and patrons of the Art Academy and Museum, who relished the magnificent views; the ceramists and painters of the Rookwood Pottery took inspiration from the surrounding flora and fauna. Nature lovers used the incline to connect with a streetcar that cruised through lovely Eden Park, perhaps culminating their trip with a visit to the zoological gardens.

In the evening, thousands of thrill-seekers rode the cable cars (some of them open-air) to view the city lights below and the stars above and to partake the sensuous pleasures of the brilliantly lighted, highly decorated, and gaudily painted Highland House. Billed as an

all-seasons resort on the brow of the Hill, here was a retreat from the hot, humid, smoky, sooty summers of the Basin that threatened disease and polluted the skies. The main building of this mammoth limestone and brick showplace, erected in 1874, remodeled in 1887, and rebuilt in 1891, had a fine, formal, two-story dining hall with a menu that rivaled Delmonico's in New York. Concert music wafted from the outdoor pavilions to enhance the diners' pleasure. There were billiard rooms on the ground floor; a balcony on the second floor accommodated private parties. On the east side, a canopied summer garden gave way to the Grand Esplanade overlook. Near the main house, facing Celestial Street, the Belvedere concert hall often featured Theodore Thomas, the nationally renowned and beloved American conductor.

A large wood pavilion surrounded by beer gardens stood nearby, where casually dressed crowds of all "classes" and nationalities enjoyed light operas. This pavilion had a bowling alley, wine cellar, and a brewery in the basement.

Many reasons have been given for the demise of Highland House and the city's other similar entertainment complexes of that era. Certainly, the invention of the automobile made an impact, as did Sunday closing laws, prohibition threats, and the general wear and tear such a facility must endure. The resort changed hands, and as culture bowed to sport it was leased to the Fair Play Athletic Club. Political groups held meetings and conventions, leading to debates that turned into fistfights—which were also popular for a time—but eventually the facility fell into disrepair and complete disfavor. It was razed in 1895.

Moving from its original site at the Rookwood railroad crossing on Riverside Drive, the Mount Adams pottery was built by Maria Longworth in 1892 next to the Highland House, across from Sterling

Glass and on the site of a fireworks factory that had burned down. (By this time the resort was already on the skids.) Rookwood was the first major American industry owned and operated by a woman and, from the beginning, women and men of various ethnic backgrounds fashioned exquisite fine art pieces out of the red, yellow, and brown Ohio River clay. They used no printing patterns and made no mass-market reproductions of what would become some of the world's most cherished signed and decorated pieces.

During the next 50 years, the Rookwood Pottery garnered honors throughout the world, particularly for the rare Tiger's Eye glaze. Highest awards at the Paris International Expositions of 1889 and 1900 and at the World's Columbian Exposition in Chicago in 1893 resulted in 24 foreign museums acquiring pieces. Many of these pieces are still intact in museums such as the Victoria and Albert Museum in London; the Musée National de Céramique, Sèvres, France; and the Museum of Art and Industry in Hamburg, Germany. Cherished by Greater Cincinnatians is the lavish and outstanding permanent exhibit in the Cincinnati Art Museum—the largest collection available to the public. The Smithsonian Institution in Washington, D.C., houses the second largest display.

Of the great structures that once dominated Mount Adams, only Rookwood remains. Today, The Rookwood is a restaurant where you can dine in a kiln and highlight your meal by studying the large display case of fine pottery that includes pieces by Edward Hurley, Kataro Shirayamadani, Albert Valentien, and Maria Longworth Nichols herself. Next door, from the tables at the sparkling Celestial restaurant in the Highland Towers, diners can still marvel at the daytime and nighttime scenes above and below the precipice that have continued to captivate Cincinnatians and visitors to the city for more than a century.

mount adams

Walk No. 4

2.3 miles

Science Stroll

IN THIS TOUR, the walker traverses the oldest, and still the most popular, societal route from the city to Mount Adams's most historical knoll. It begins downtown near Procter & Gamble; the company's formal garden is outstanding any time of year, but best in early May when the wisteria vines on the pergolas are laden with elongated clusters of perfected purple flowers. After safely traversing I-71 by way of modern steps and overpass, the walker is guided on an indirect but fascinating journey to the culmination of Monastery and Celestial Streets, offering stimulating views of the perfectly sited, painstakingly designed Rookwood Pottery en route. The ruins of the Mount Adams Incline are examined as an archeological diversion. The biology lesson includes the rainbow-colored snails seen in and around the stone retaining walls. And for geological thrills, the site of the nation's most expensive landslide is studied; it becomes quite apparent why experts nicknamed Cincinnati "Landslide city, USA."

Park on 4th, 5th, or 6th Streets between Broadway and Main Streets, or at a two-hour meter around Procter & Gamble.

- Make your way to the outstanding twin-towered plaza on 5th between Sycamore and Broadway Streets; step up to enjoy the horticultural display.
- Follow 5th Street east, past the towers, turning left on Sentinel Street. Here you can gaze up at Mount Adams to pinpoint

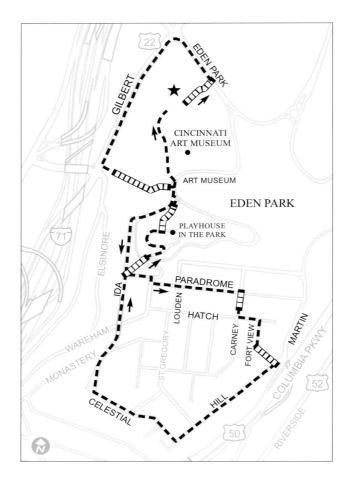

the Tudor-style Rookwood Pottery building; the area where the Mount Adams Incline cut into the hillside below; and Holy Cross Monastery. Highland Towers, with its Celestial restaurant inside (tinted windows), occupies the same spot where the huge Highland House resort sat, over a century ago (see discussion in Walk No. 3).

- Continue down Sentinel Street to the steel and concrete **6th Street Steps.** Climb these 67 risers to tramp along the wide viaduct sidewalk over I-71. As you cross the expressway, you get a fine perspective of the cement columns, three to seven feet in diameter, marking the site of the nation's most expensive landslide, set off in 1973 by excavations for the I-471 ramps—$22 million worth of slippery mud. In the late 1970s, the columns were anchored up to 120 feet into the hillside to shore up Mount Adams.
- Go up the stout-handrailed ramp on the left, which is the only way to continue, to Monastery Street.
- Left on Monastery. Right on Baum Street.

mount adams

- Left on Oregon Street, curving around the intersection where the walkway to the **Celestial Street Steps** tempts you to digress (to Walk No. 1). Excellent view here of the city's riverfront sports and entertainment complexes. More incline ruins are seen mid-Oregon Street, on the right. There were no structures underneath the city inclines, but people did live in homes on the streets the inclines crossed. A staircase (no longer visible) known as the **4th Street Steps** ran from Loch Street to Celestial Street, which served residents of Kilgour, Baum, and Oregon Streets.
- Right on Monastery. This steep street is one of the first hills ascended by runners participating in the Cincinnati Recreation Commission's "Seven Hills Run." For 20 years, runners have huffed and puffed up and down Mount Adams, Mount Auburn, and Fairmount hillocks to peak out in Price Hill.
- Right on Celestial Street.
- Continuing down the sidewalk, note the ubiquitous rooks (an Old World bird resembling the North American crow)

perched on the original stone gateposts guarding the Rookwood Pottery. During the late autumn migration, it becomes apparent why these birds were given this honor.

- Walk to the large parking lot at the corner of Celestial and
  Celestial. Walk south through the parking lot to the cliff edge
  overlooking the Ohio River. Below on the hillside are the remains of the Mount Adams Incline. Next door, the Highland Towers apartment building is on the site of the former
  Highland House, which serviced the top of the incline. Turn
  around and face the hillside above. Gazing across Celestial
  Street, you can see Holy Cross Monastery, now occupying
  the site where the Cincinnati Observatory once sat.

- Walk west along the circumference of the parking lot in back of
  The Rockwood restaurant and office building. You will have

spectacular views of downtown, northern
Kentucky, and the Ohio River. You might
be able to spot your parked car.

- Return to the corner of Celestial and
  Celestial, and read the metal plaque
  of the Mount Adams Preservation
  Association. Walk west on Celestial
  to the corner of Ida and Monastery.

- Doris Day fans will want to ascend
  Monastery one block higher to view
  the attractive structure at 1033
  Monastery. During the 1930s, this
  was the Hessler Studio of Dancing,
  Miss Kappelhoff's favorite school.
  She rode four streetcars from her
  Evanston home to get here.

- At the southwest corner of Monastery
  Street and the Ida Street Viaduct,

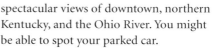

descend the seven flights of **Monastery Street Steps.** Children attending schools in the Basin used these steps until 1885, when the first public school on Mount Adams was opened.

- Left on Wareham Drive, down and around to Van Meter Street.
- Cross Van Meter, and head down the green-fenced commuters' footbridge over I-71 to the **Court Street Steps,** Court Street side.
- Follow this sidewalk to Broadway, crossing 6th Street, continuing south to your parked car.

The Observatory

Because its outstanding history began in Mount Adams, it seems appropriate that the story of the Cincinnati Observatory should begin here, before the walker proceeds to Mount Lookout to view where the country's first giant telescope found its current resting place.

Built in 1843 and dedicated by avid astronomer John Quincy Adams, the Cincinnati Observatory housed an 11-inch Merz and Mahler refracting telescope, the largest in the United States at that time. Early astronomers viewed stars and planets during the night, but they also were keen on examining and recording weather phenomena during the day—during this time in history, no one else did it. As the industrial, polluted Cincinnati skies blacked out more and more stars and planets, it occurred to local astronomer Cleveland Abbe that weather "forecasting" might be the most important contribution the Mount Adams observatory would ever make.

Abbe requested and received financial assistance from the Cincinnati Chamber of Commerce, and in September 1869, he began issuing the nation's first daily weather bulletins. Working with the Western Union Telegraph Company, Abbe received weather bulletins from around the country, coordinated the data, and reported the information in a newspaper column. This was actually an advertising inducement; the column promoted subscriptions for the daily bulletins that the Chamber printed for $1.50 per month. Expecting fourteen cities to respond on September 1, Abbe optimistically persevered when for almost a week only Leavenworth, St. Louis, Chicago, and Minneapolis responded. By September 11, however, the official form carried data from 22 stations.

The service was particularly popular with pork slaughterhouses in Cincinnati. Advance warning of an unexpected hot spell might, for instance, be reason to cease slaughtering if cold storage was not available.

Unfortunately, not enough subscribers paid to keep the publication going for more than a year. But Abbe's enterprise gained national acclaim, and two years later, when the federal government established the United States Weather Bureau, Cleveland Abbe was appointed Chief Meteorologist.

In 1872, the Cincinnati Astronomical Society turned over its rights to the observatory to the University of Cincinnati, knowing that the station would have to be moved to a higher, cleaner atmosphere. Mount Lookout advocate John Kilgour wanted his suburb to have the honor, so he donated 13 acres and $10,000 toward a new building for the Merz and Mahler telescope.

Surrounded by evergreens and looming out of the mist on an inclement day, two single-story red brick observatories repose on a hump near the crest of Mount Lookout (seen in the Ault Park walk). The main, newer observatory has a stone portico with four columns; the roof supports the large, sheet-metal dome that houses a 16-inch telescope, purchased in 1904. The smaller domed building houses the original 11-inch telescope. Information on astronomy, the observatory, public shows, and classes may be obtained by calling (513) 321-5186 (University of Cincinnati Observatory).

mount adams

MOUNT AUBURN

Stairways: After years of neglect this plan recognizes the fact that the steps remain as a vital feature of the hillside district. The first priority should be to maintain the steps to allow them to be usable and safe. The additional improvements of small scale pedestrian lights, low deciduous and flowering plantings, viewing platforms, and crosswalk improvements would enhance and develop this fine resource as would new steps where they are needed. . . . Landscaping pathways can visually and functionally link larger open spaces to neighborhoods and increase personal mobility. . . . The most significant element in the rehabilitation of the steps is the work done at the crossing point between the stairs-path and the roadway. This point is to be treated as a crosswalk, with special paving at the sidewalk, lighting and markings. . . . This work is a vital concern to the residents of Mount Auburn, because the steps really get used.

Cincinnati Planning Commission,
Mount Auburn: Prospect Hill
Historic Conservation Plan *(1981)*

Walk No. 5

2.3 miles

Prospect Hill

WHEN YOU ENTER Liberty Hill from Over-the-Rhine and ascend into the square-mile Prospect Hill National Historic District, you cannot help but detect the heartbeat of the 200-year-old City of Cincinnati. Everyday folks, most of German descent, lived in the picturesque brick townhouses erected here in the early 1800s; men and women who worked in the city and helped make it great. The sole mansion marking the peak of Liberty Hill belonged to George and Mary Alicia Pendleton; he was a U.S. Senator and founder of the Civil Service Commission; she was the youngest daughter of Francis Scott Key, composer of the national anthem. The area was called the "Northern Liberties" then, referring to the fact that until 1849 the City's taxation laws ended at Corporation Alley. Liberty Street and Liberty Hill were named accordingly. Dr. Daniel Drake, founder of the University of Cincinnati medical college, referred to Prospect Hill as "Mount Poverty" because when he moved into a log cabin on what is now Milton Street, it was quite rural and he

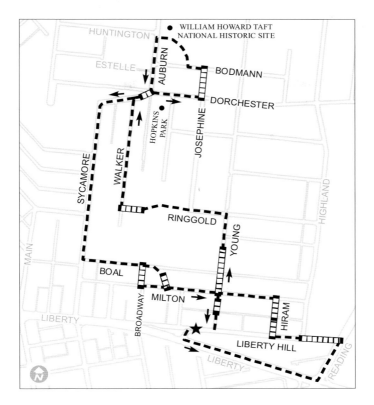

was quite penniless. Investment in real estate was considered the safest and possibly the most profitable investment, and many of Mount Auburn's streets and steps—Young, Mansfield, Slack, Boal —reflect the names of early investors. Elijah Slack, Robert Boal, and William Price (who may have been related to the developers of Price Hill) practiced medicine. Although Prospect Hill has gone through many rough periods, today it is once again gentrified. This walk circumambulates the entire Historic District and samples a few of the British settlers' mansions atop Mount Auburn; it peaks at "Pill Hill," the site of Christ Hospital.

   Park on Liberty Hill or Liberty Street between Young and Main.
 • Walk east on Liberty Street. Turn left onto Reading Road and
       walk about one block north to the **City Steps**. Ascend the
       steps up Liberty Hill to the intersection of Liberty Hill and
       Highland Avenue.
 • Cross the street and walk downhill; after passing a few houses
       you will soon encounter the beautiful **Hiram Street Steps**.
       Ascend, crossing Corporation Alley, to Milton Street.
 • Left on Milton for about one block. Right on the **Young Street
       Steps**. Notice the attractive cul-de-sac at the bottom section
       of the **Young Street Steps**; summertime block parties are
       held in this cozy niche.

- Pause to take in the view at Boal. There are about 100 **Young Street Step** risers to go!
- At the pinnacle of the **Young Street Steps,** continue ahead on Young Street. But before you do, take note of the view and the broken monument at the peak of the steps. During the mid-1880s, the Hamilton County Courthouse was destroyed by fire. The only thing that survived was a spectacular ornate marble archway, which was moved to this site. It stood here until 1965, when all but this column base was toppled in a car accident. Perhaps someday, with a little help from the public sector, the arch will reappear in all its majestic beauty.
- Left on Ringgold Street to Josephine Street.
- Follow the blacktop path through the woods, one block, to the **Ringgold Street Steps.**
- Right on Walker Avenue; left first, if you want to peek at another vista.

- Right on Sycamore.
- Climb the fancy **Auburn Avenue Steps** to Dorchester Avenue. The two-and-a-half-story brick home at this corner belonged to Henry Martin, owner of the Mount Auburn Cable Railway (not inclined). In an odd religious ritual, Martin transferred the title of his railway every Saturday night and resumed ownership every Monday morning to observe the Sabbath.
- Proceed east on Dorchester for about two blocks or detour through Hopkins Park. Take note of the checkerboard-topped tables around the pavilion. In the spring the daffodils along the wrought iron fence are spectacular. Exit back onto Dorchester.
- Left at Josephine Street to ascend the **Josephine Street Steps**.
- Left on Bodman Avenue. Look straight ahead: the fine mansion sitting on Mount Auburn's highest hillock formerly housed Adam Riddle, a prominent attorney.
- Follow the cement path on the right to view the brightly painted William Howard Taft National Shrine, birthplace of our twenty-seventh president. It is the smallest and least visited national park in the United States (open 10 A.M. to 4 P.M. daily). Stop in!
- Left on Auburn Avenue. The few **Estelle Street Steps** can be viewed across Auburn. Descend the second set of very wide

Auburn Avenue Steps across Sycamore from the fancy ones you ascended.

- Begin your scenic descent of Sycamore Street.
- Two-thirds of the way down on the left is Boal Street. Walk east on Boal. You have two choices: Descend the elegant **Broadway Street Steps** to Milton Street. Proceed to the well-kept neighborhood park on the right. In this friendly park— complete with benches, game tables, colorful vegetation, and a romantic archway blooming with roses in the summer— walk through the arch and down the steps to Milton.
- Turn left on Milton and walk about two blocks to Young Street. Turn right into the cul-de-sac of Young Street and descend the steps to Corporation Alley. Continue on Young Street to Liberty Hill and your parked car.

Caroline Williams

Although many great artists have found beauty and inspiration in the Cincinnati hills and valleys, one of the best-loved artists had the vision to immortalize one of the city's greatest assets: the Cincinnati steps. Caroline Williams's remarkable contribution was a book entitled *Cincinnati Steeples, Streets, and Steps*—a record of her incomparable pen-and-ink illustrations—that she designed, wrote, edited, printed, and published herself on a hand press in her own home.

Born in Covington in 1908, Caroline Williams's roots embraced Indiana, Ohio, and Kentucky, qualifying her as a tri-state artisan in the truest sense. She did not marry or have children, but she had an abiding love and interest in family. One of the many projects of her adult life was compiling genealogical information, resulting in a family-tree portrait that hung on a door in her home and was about the same size as the door itself.

Her father, Carll (C. B.) Williams, art director for the *Cincinnati Enquirer*, was almost deaf, but he was an expert lip-reader with a capacious sense of humor. C. B. Williams's work as a newspaper illustrator demanded an extraordinary talent, from knowledge about politics and crime to cartooning and current events, because line drawings were used far more often than photographs during that era.

C. B. married Mary Teal, a strong-willed woman supportive of the talents of her husband and her three children. Caroline was the youngest and the only one to follow in her father's footsteps. When C. B. moved from staff artist to director, the family bought a home in College Hill, where in the summer he conducted an art workshop in a backyard tent. No doubt Caroline's love of creating in the outdoors flowered in this encouraging setting. C. B. belonged to the Cincinnati Art Club and counted among his friends Frank Duveneck and E. T. Hurley. Hurley frequently visited the summer workshop, influencing and cultivating Caroline's self esteem and professionalism. She attended Hughes High School and studied one year at the University of Cincinnati and two years at the Art Academy. Two years spent in New York at the Art Students League were concentrated on portraiture.

When Caroline was 20 years old her beloved father died. The next year brought the Great Depression; soon after, it was obvious that commissions from painting portraits would not provide a living for her and her mother. Her siblings had married and had families of their own. Hired by the *Enquirer*, Williams began her spectacular career. Initially, she pitched in wherever she was needed, but it did not take long for her editor to recognize her talent. Caroline had an ability to recreate the city's architecture in a line drawing that was stunning in its impact. Each line had meaning, grace, art, purpose —and heart. She drew historic buildings, new buildings, churches, and stairs—structures set in places where each had enhanced rather than destroyed its natural surroundings. She drew tenement houses where life superseded the setting. Although she fervently believed that the city would be best served by creatively mixing the old with the modern and by paying more attention to the needs of the poor, Williams apparently never considered voicing these ideas via an overt political platform. Instead, she opted to express these messages, based on firsthand observations, quietly but boldly through her art.

Assigned a weekly space to illustrate a favorite "Spot in Cincinnati," she first sketched a Liberty Hill skyline; it appeared in November 1932. Soon Cincinnatians were looking forward to her "column." Many clipped the drawings to compile scrapbooks. (As a child, I sought out certain sites and compared them with the drawings to solve the mystery of exactly where Williams had sat when she made her drawings.) A sentence or two accompanied each drawing, revealing Caroline's unique ability to communicate meaningful information in a few well-chosen words.

Williams kept her personal life private. She met her lifelong best friend, Dorothy Caldwell, through a World War II organization called the Committee to Defend America. The two volunteered for Red Cross duty and served by driving blood donors back to their homes; training for this job included scheduled maintenance of the ambulance.

For years, Williams longed to buy her grandfather's log cabin in Metamora, Indiana, but the opportunity never presented itself. When the Caldwell family decided to buy land in Burlington, Kentucky, Caroline accompanied Dorothy on a scouting trip and spotted a two-story log house, exactly the sort she desired. She and her mother purchased the 52-acre property and set up a homestead. Caroline was a Renaissance woman long before the word "liberated" was linked to "woman," maintaining as high a standard for her home life as she did in her career. It was in this domicile that Caroline and her mother, who lived into her eighties, would express every facet of their rugged individualism. They repaired and decorated the home; raised bees, goats, pond fish, and flowers; and hired a farmer to grow vegetables. They kept a dog, usually a poodle.

During her 47 years with the *Enquirer*, the paper published two volumes of her sketches, *The City on Seven Hills* (1938), and *Mirror Landmarks of Cincinnati* (1939); Doubleday published *Cincinnati Scenes* (1962) and *Louisville Scenes* (1971). In 1941 she designed and drew a stylized map of Cincinnati for Closson's Christmas sale. The next year Williams and Caldwell drove to Quebec, where she sketched and later etched impressions of the French towns for a Closson's exhibition. One of Caroline's more famous collaborations was the production of commemorative plates bearing Cincinnati scenes for Newstedt-Loring Andrews. Produced by Wedgwood, the plates have been issued once a year since 1968, and many are collector's items.

Of the Cincinnati steps Williams depicted in her illustrations, many have disappeared or have been altered for the worse, such as those in the *Hughes Street Steps,* the *Lang Street Steps,* and the *Top of Sycamore Hill.* Whatever steps we still possess in Cincinnati may well be the result of Caroline's cherishing them during decades of vast upheaval, a task that is now left to those who agree with her assessment of treasures worth keeping.

Caroline's pen was never in error. Each stroke perfectly captured the spirit of the scene. No phony folderols were added, no selfish interpretation. The result was a work of art so genuine in its clarity that the memory could not put it down.

Caroline Williams died in her sleep in her log house in 1988.

Walk No. 6

2.4 miles

The Main Street Steps

ALTHOUGH MANY OF its old stairways are fully or partially destroyed, Mount Auburn still has more step risers than any other
Cincinnati suburb, and this walk points out more historic public
stairways than any other walk in this guidebook. If one were to
speculate where the early residents built the first lengthy flights of
Cincinnati steps, this would be the place. Mount Auburn also has
the distinction of possessing Cincinnati's lengthiest stairway—the
ever-escalating **Main Street Steps**—as Main Street, one of the city's
hubs of great music, taverns, and microbreweries, climaxes in a
stairway to the stars. On the other hand, the **Gage Street Steps** are
downright scary. Neighborhoods visited during this strenuous trek
are excellent to shabby, but they are all stimulating. From the heart-
pounding climb to the potentially hazardous descent, the boast
"I Conquered the Main Street Steps" would not entirely be spoken
in jest. It is believed that Charles Dickens was standing somewhere
along these Mount Auburn bluffs when he described the city "lying
in an amphitheatre of hills," forming a "picture of remarkable beauty."
Quite so. Dickens, who had few good things to say about the New
World, lavishly praised two cities: Boston and Cincinnati. Because
the Mount Auburn steps were built for the specific purpose of connecting the Over-the-Rhine neighborhoods to the heights of Mount
Auburn, it is appropriate to begin this walk on 14th Street in Over-
the-Rhine, just southwest of the commemorative carillon gateway.

Park on 13th or 14th Streets between Sycamore and Broadway
Streets.

- Walk east on 13th or 14th. Turn left at Broadway, Spring, or
  Pendleton. Liberty Street can be accessed by the **Pendleton
  Street Steps**, the **Spring Street Steps**, or the **Broadway Street
  Steps**—the latter being the friendliest.
- The old school site, on 13th Street, has been associated with
  education in Cincinnati since William Woodward and
  his wife Abigail Cutter donated the land for a college.
  William Howard Taft, a member of the graduating class of
  1874, laid the cornerstone for the present stone, brick, and
  terracotta structure dating back to 1920. It was first the
  home of Woodward High School, then Cutter Junior High

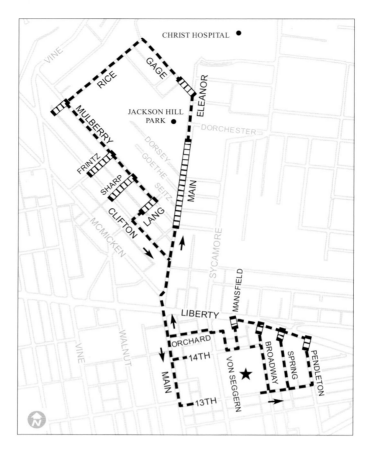

and, most recently, the School for Creative and Performing
Arts. Now the building houses administrative offices.

- Climb the **Broadway Street Steps** to Liberty Street; turn left.
  Higher **Broadway Street Steps** are visited in the Prospect
  Hill walk; they can be seen from here. Also take notice, at
  the bottom of Liberty Hill, of the four-story First District
  School, one of the oldest examples of public school archi-
  tecture in Cincinnati, renovated into apartments.

- Left on the **Mansfield Street Steps**.
- Right on 14th Street.
- Right on Von Seggern Alley; cross Sycamore Street to continue west on Orchard Street.
- Right on Main Street; cross Liberty Street. Note the churches, taverns, restaurants, and interesting shops in this busy area.
- Continue north on Main Street, past the Rothenberg Preparatory Academy, to Mulberry Street.
- Introducing the **Main Street Steps**! Hundreds of them. The phrase "oxygen sickness" has been jokingly used in reference to the ascent you have before you. Onward!
- Although they were once underneath the Main Street Incline, Seitz, Goethe, and Dorsey Streets now cross the **Main Street Steps**. These "landings" give you an opportunity to turn around and revel in the optimal views of old Cincinnati: the red brick homes and tenements of Over-the-Rhine and the outstanding Samuel Hannaford architecture.
- Jackson Hill Park provides a restful pause and an opportunity to muse about the past. The park is located at the top of the Main Street or Mount Auburn Incline, the ruins of which can be seen over the side of the hill. Lookout House and German Park once occupied the Jackson Hill Park site. During the late 1800s, the spot was a hub of activity, but when the incline and resort were demolished at the turn of the century, Mother Nature reclaimed the grounds. In 1909, the city leased the property to the Jackson family, Cincinnati nurserymen for many decades, to operate a tree and floral

nursery, which they did until 1925. During that time, the
spot became known as "Jackson's Hill" and it has been
ever since.
- Forward on Eleanor Place.
- Left to descend the oft-photographed, precipitous Gage
  Street Steps.
- Move ahead on Gage to Rice Street; turn left.
- Left on Mulberry Street. (Turning right will bring you to Vine
  Street and the foot of the Vine Street Steps, which lead to
  the Ohio Avenue Steps and Bellevue Park. When the trees
  are bare, the steps can be seen in the distance decorating
  the hillside.)
- As you follow Mulberry Street back to Main Street through a
  neighborhood in transition, you will view, on the south and
  sometimes north sides, the secluded Rice Street Steps, the
  Frintz Street Steps, and the Sharp Alley Steps.
- Continue on Mulberry to Lang Street and turn right to descend
  the Lang Street Steps. Turn left on Clifton, and right on
  Main Street. Walk south on Main to 13th or 14th Street and
  your parked car.

The Mount Auburn Incline

Constrained by a semicircle of inaccessible hills, the growing metrop-
olis of Cincinnati was bursting its seams by the mid-1800s. Residents
of the congested Basin and Over-the-Rhine neighborhoods needed
a way to escape the foul air, filth, and fumes and command the spectacular views the woodsy hilltops had to offer.

Rail transportation was already popular, giving way to the idea
that perhaps rails could be attached to the slopes. But although that
idea and many other harebrained schemes failed to flower, the an-
swer would be a railway of sorts—a combination railway and eleva-
tor. In 1872, the first Cincinnati incline was built directly north of

the head of Main Street, on Mulberry Street, by a private firm, the Cincinnati Inclined-Plane Railway Company. The Mount Auburn Incline, also known as the Main Street Incline, was 960 slant-feet in length and steeper at the bottom.

It was an immediate success. Three additional inclines were planned and built during the 1870s, followed by the building of homes, taverns, shops, and roads on the sides and tops of the conquered hills.

Eventually, the rectangular, grand Lookout House resort was erected next to the "Celestial Depot" at the top of the hill, in what was then known as German Park. Its concert hall, restaurant, saloon, and theater were not nearly as lavish as the Highland House on Mount Adams, so the management brought in carnival sideshows, fireworks displays, hot-air balloonists, yodelers, and in one inhumane extravaganza, a dwarf white whale imprisoned in a huge tank of salt water. The unfortunate creature lived only one miserable month under those conditions; however, in a bizarre effort to extend its successful run, the proprietors embalmed the mammal. At this point, the whale wreaked revenge. The pickling process was a dismal failure, and efforts to get rid of the corpse and the odor lasted several weeks (and probably cost a pretty penny).

The Mount Auburn Incline was the first—and only—Cincinnati incline to experience a tragic accident. A few minutes after noon on October 15, 1889, the brakes failed at the top and the cable broke. The eight passengers preparing to get off could not, and the car careened downward, sideswiping but not seriously damaging the downward car on the other track. Both cars stayed on the rails, but the doomed car hit the bottom of the incline at full speed. The sides collapsed, and the roof flew off and crashed into homes on Mulberry Street, and then ricocheted into Main Street where it flattened out "like a sheet of newspaper." Only one passenger survived.

Although the damage was repaired, faith in the Mount Auburn Incline was forever destroyed. In addition, the construction of Vine Street as the major artery into Mount Auburn, accommodating the faster and more convenient electric streetcar, caused the incline to decline in popularity. In 1899, after 27 years—the shortest life of the five Cincinnati inclines and the only one closed before 1900—the Mount Auburn Incline was no more. As a result of the tragedy, special precautions were enforced on the other three existing inclines and the one to follow, allowing Cincinnati's incline history to boast a rather remarkable safety record.

It is believed that the concrete **Main Street Steps** were built into the incline right-of-way by the Works Projects Administration (WPA) in the early 1940s.

PRICE'S HILLS

Certain stairways in the city—the **Broadway Steps**, the **Earnshaw Steps**, and the **Denver Avenue Steps**, for instance —were repaired in the late 1980s by City Maintenance Workers. These six or seven men were very capable and were proud of the work they did. Other privately owned construction companies left their signatures in the wet cement, so they decided to do the same. "Public Step Brothers" and the date, inside a star, was to be their trademark. Of course, the City made them stop. But it didn't take away their pride in a job well done.

William M. Gay,
City of Cincinnati Engineering Technician

Walk No. 7

2.2 miles

Mount Hope

WITHIN THE BOUNDARIES of the Price Hill suburb, several major hills and ravines are interconnected. This terrific trek begins with a climb up an outstanding set of steps in Lower Price Hill, continues into East Price Hill, completely traverses the historically formidable Mount Hope or "Price's Hill" as it was also known, and showcases the superlative steps of Sedamsville. Although many famous Price Hill pioneers once resided atop this modest mountain, few remnants remain to commemorate this glittering past. Two stops are mandatory: the Moore-Knight Home at 716 Mount Hope Avenue, recently designated a historic site and the only residence in the city to be so honored; and Olden View Park, the location of the only Cincinnati incline honored by memorial plaques. Colonel Robert Moore, who married Ann Eliza Price, granddaughter of Evans Price, was one of the city's most public-spirited and charitable citizens; he became mayor of Cincinnati in 1877. Moore aided Civil War soldiers in getting pensions, and his custom of conducting military services at the graves of his comrades preceded the formal establishment of Memorial Day by Congress. Noteworthy for their exceptional achievements in education, the Knight family includes generations of teachers and scholars. Among them were Alphia Troy, one of the

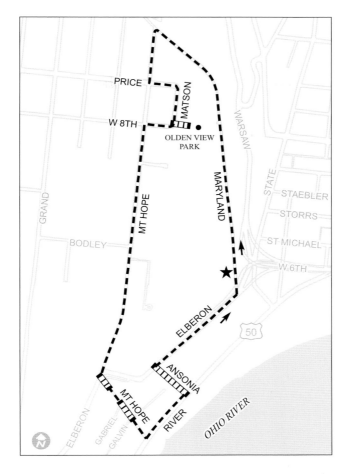

first black teachers in Cincinnati; her daughter Laura Troy Knight, principal of Jackson Colony, which was part of the Harriet Beecher Stowe School downtown; and granddaughter Laura Knight Turner, who graduated from the University of Cincinnati at age eighteen.

Park on Maryland Avenue at the bottom of the hill.

- Maryland Hill is a steep avenue of many surprises; it once went straight through to Mount Hope Avenue, passing under the incline. Head up, catching aerie glimpses of downtown and river, and a few more closed stairways. Roll a "brainball," the fruit of the osage orange tree, down the hill if you can find one.

- Faint ruins of the incline may be seen on both sides of the hill. When the trees are bare you can orient yourself by pinpointing the Queen's Tower on the hilltop. Continue along the woodsy blacktop path (still Maryland Avenue) at the end of this residential area.

- Left onto Mount Hope Road.

- Left on Price Avenue. Right on Matson Place.

- Continue past the Queen's Tower apartments where Prima-vista, an Italian restaurant, offers the same stunning city view as the park next door but far more elegantly.
- Descend the **Olden View Park Steps**. Brass etchings are mounted into the semicircular wall here, remembrances of the incline and Hilltop House. Pause to absorb this Best of the West public view at the precipice—elevation 840 feet—and the history. From this point the grand West 8th Street viaduct clearly delineates the early settlers' daily route. With half of 8th Street far below and half of 8th Street behind you, it is evident how the Price Hill Incline linked the two. Cannons rested here during the Civil War when the city was placed under martial law. On the right is the Incline Public House. It opened in 2012 at the same location as the original Price Hill House, which was opened by William Price in 1874, staying in operation until the 1930s.
- Head back to Mount Hope Road via 8th Street; turn left. But before you do, take note of the red brick Masonic Lodge building that some believe is a landmark worth saving. In addition, Raymond Dandridge, African-American poet, lived at the northwest corner of 8th and Chateau, one block down. A polio victim in his early teens, the handsome Dandridge was bedridden, selling coal by telephone to make a living. His *Penciled Poems* (1917) contains a moving poem about Price Hill, although it is written in the dialect black writers had to foster to please publishers.
- 716 Mount Hope Avenue is the Moore-Knight home, perched on the cliff, off the road. A magnificent structure in a magnificent setting; coach house in front.
- Continue down, down, down.
- Cross Elberon Avenue at the bottom of Mount Hope Avenue. This is a challenging two-wheeler curve. Descend the first 18 **Mount Hope Avenue Steps**.

- Follow Mount Hope Avenue down to Gabriel Avenue at the edge of the woods, where you will see about 65 more of the same steps; descend to Galvin Avenue. Continue down a few more steps along Mount Hope Avenue to River Road to enter another old, historic area of Cincinnati: Sedamsville.
- Left on River Road for about two blocks.
- Left on the first of 120 shining **Ansonia Avenue Steps**. Finish your climb.
- Right on Elberon Avenue, to Maryland Avenue, and your parked car.

From Horsecar to Hilltop House

The Price name in Cincinnati began with Evans and Sarah Pierce Price, who were of Welsh descent. Evans was a merchant who amassed a fortune in land in the western hills, but a boating accident left him unable to manage his holdings. His son Rees inherited the responsibilities of an insolvent estate, yet he too became a successful investor and prospered in the family brick-making and lumber businesses at what is now 8th and State. In 1824, Rees married Sarah, daughter of Judge Isaac B. Matson, and the couple had eight children. Sons John and William oversaw construction of the incline and much of the

efficient system of transportation that finally enabled adventurous local pioneers to Go West. The names of two daughters were exploited on the incline's original passenger cars, "Highland Mary" and "Lily-of-the-Valley."

The Price Hill Incline was Cincinnati's second incline, built two years after the Mount Auburn Incline. It was twice as impressive as its predecessor, being double-planed; that is, two separate sets of tracks with four cars going up and down an 80-foot width of hillside. One side for passengers; one side for freight: three or four heavily loaded wagons with teams of horses. This unique feature eventually led to the mistaken assumption that Cincinnati produced six inclines when in fact there were five. The Price Hill Incline passed over two streets, Warsaw and Maryland Avenues, requiring four bridges with stone piers and massive wood beams. Beginning at 8th and Glenway, the track rose some 800 slant-feet; it was a five-minute trip. There were no steps alongside, but there were steps leading from Maryland Avenue to Mount Hope Avenue, and from Warsaw Avenue to Maryland Avenue.

At the time of the incline's construction, the Mill Creek was still proving to be a problem for pedestrians and travelers on horseback. An unreliable floating toll bridge, followed by a series of wooden bridges periodically ravaged by flood and fire, spanned the treacherous creek bottoms from the Basin to the precipitous western hillside. And if that wasn't enough, bears, panthers, wildcats, and wolves were on the prowl. Citizens referred to the passage as "Dead Man's Crossing." William and John solved the problem by gathering a fleet of horse-drawn carriages with armed drivers called "Price's Chariots," to taxi their clientele to and from the incline.

They also designed a resort. The Price family had proud, estimable fantasies for the enterprise that would crown what was now commonly referred to as Price's Hill. They did not want the kind of uninhibited alcoholic revelry that went on at competitors' establishments. In fact, William Price hoped to set an example of healthy living and self-control that would discourage alcohol consumption throughout the growing community. He decided Hilltop House would be dry.

The station house erected had a 100-foot cupola-topped observation tower; it also housed art and music halls. Landscaped gardens with gazebo and rustic furniture gave way to an awesome, lengthy, overlook terrace. The grand dining room seated 1,000 diners whose palates were perfectly satisfied while their thirst was slaked by lemonade, ginger beer, and milk.

For a time the plan worked. The novelty of being able to head to the western heights so quickly was worth the sacrifice, even for the jolly Germans who preferred beer to any other liquid, including water. But soon it turned sour. Saloons at the bottom of the hill put up "Last Chance" signs—an announcement increasingly heeded as passengers arrived or waited in line to board the incline. The thirsty visited again on the return trip; the alcoholic influence was not avoided and the Price brothers lost money to boot. Worse yet, Price's Hill became the town laughing-stock, now referred to as "Buttermilk Mountain."

The Price family gave into public demand. The tower was removed from the neglected concert hall so the resort could become an indoor-outdoor beer garden of the first order. Rechristened Price Hill House, and the original site of Stricker's Grove picnic grounds, it stayed alive until 1938.

The Price Hill Incline had but one serious mishap, and that to two teams of horses, one pulling a load of sand, the other manure. When the cable snapped at the top, one lucky driver landed in sand, and the other (not so lucky) landed in manure; both were saved.

By 1941, roads were the preferred mode of travel, and weeds had overtaken the nearly forgotten freight side of the incline. Passengers, however, kept their side almost as popular on the day the incline closed as the day it opened. In 1893, the grandiose concrete 8th Street viaduct with its art deco look and tony boulevard lighting had renewed the incline's novelty; 8th and State remained a hub of activity as a shopping district, streetcar transfer point, and "tourist" attraction for decades. By 1941, however, the incline was badly in need of repairs, as a result of damage from fire and landslides. When city inspectors decided to tear down the incline and substitute a shuttle bus service, Price Hill residents went into action to protest the decision; the East Price Hill Incline Association was formed for that very purpose. They begged the city to rethink and reinvest. On July 31, 1943, a rotting crosstie caused a rail spread and a car jumped the track. No one was injured but the incline was shut down. The Price Hill Incline had proudly served Cincinnatians for almost 70 years.

Walk No. 8

1.6 miles

Mount Echo

MOUNT ECHO PARK and its surrounds are the primary foci of this civic-minded East Price Hill excursion, as we single out park stairs built by Franklin Roosevelt's Works Projects Administration (WPA). In 1986, at great cost, the Cincinnati Park District completely remodeled Mount Echo Park's formal outlook and stabilized the slipping hillside, and this construction, too, draws our attention. The Mount Hope overlooks, from about 825 feet above sea level, offer expansive views of downtown Cincinnati, the railroad yards, the Mill Creek valley, and the impressive "S" bend of the Ohio River. Make no mistake; this is no ordinary vista. Mount Echo offers the best skyline perspective of Cincinnati's downtown on the Ohio side of the river. The cliffs resonate sound, particularly train rumblings and boat whistles echoing off the mountain's face. Mount Echo was once known as Bold Face Hill in honor of the chief whose tribe made its home here. Further exploration of this area is recommended.

Drive into Mount Echo Park, turning right at the first drive (before the river overlook and dance pavilion). Continue to the end and park in the lot between the softball diamond and the basketball/tennis courts.

- Follow the blacktop-to-cement path at the east side of the basketball/tennis courts to Crestline Avenue.

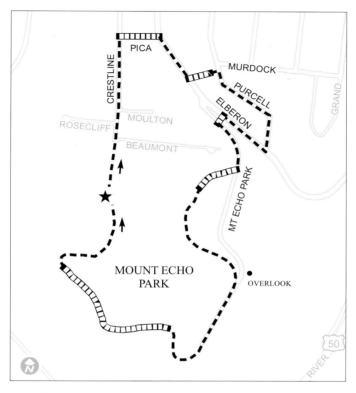

- Follow Crestline Avenue about three blocks; turn right on the charming **Pica Street Steps** to Elberon Avenue.
- Cross Elberon Avenue; go right.
- Climb the slightly listing **Murdock Avenue Steps**.
- Right on Purcell Avenue. Three East Price Hill tiers can be glimpsed from this location; the cute homes along Elberon, Purcell, and Murdock show a neighborhood in the process of reclaiming its luster.
- Cross Elberon again and head up to reenter the park on foot, in a grandiose fashion: Ascend the ornamental **Mount Echo Park Steps**, built by the WPA in 1939. The three-tiered view improves from this vantage point.
- Follow the sidewalk into the park.
- Right on the gracious fieldstone stairway winding up the hillside to the WPA shelter house, dated 1940. The spectacular view here creates a unique photograph of the city, framed on the top by the scalloped edge of the shelterhouse roof, and on the bottom by the WPA stone wall.
- Waltz on over to the marble-columned pavilion. Take in the magnificent cliffside overlook from several vantage points, including the Price Hill Garden Club crescent seat. (If you want to experience a surprisingly satisfying acoustical

phenomenon, step down into the seating area. Stand on the first step in front of the crescent seat, facing the seat and aligning your feet with the drain. Say something to the seat and enjoy the magic.) Pause to read the "East Price Hill" Bicentennial Commission plaque. Step up to the marble-columned pavilion; this is one of only two city parks where dances are held (the other is Ault Park).

- Follow the drive to the end, past the playground, where an industrial yet pleasant overlook awaits.
- Cross to the small picnic area on your right; head toward the edge of the woods and search for the opening to the ravine path that will take you back to your starting point. It's not far. Aha, there it is.

price's hills

- The ravine path is a step-medley that connects two park hill-ocks. A tribute to the ingeniousness and conservation skills of the park maintenance workers, the original limestone and sandstone steps of all shapes and sizes, some of them mossy, lichened, or fossilized, have been interlaced and reinforced with recycled cement steps, tree roots, and wood four-by-fours. The stairway opens a path through beds of glorious spring wildflowers, preserving them while presenting them.
- Cross the footbridge.
- End up in a grassy section of a park trail; turn right, toward the road.
- Head up to the basketball/tennis courts and your parked car.

The Men Who Built the Steps

The story of Cincinnati's superb parks, their splendid furnishings and steps, began in 1817 when the city acquired the downtown land for what is now called Piatt Park. Eden Park's genesis was 1859, followed by Burnet Woods in 1872. With this foundation, the city's park system burgeoned in 1907 under the vision of Kansas City resident George Kessler. Kessler, a protégé of Frederick Law Olmsted, had successfully designed parks in Baltimore, Cleveland, and Kansas City. Hired by the City of Cincinnati to generate an overall park plan, Kessler's advice was simple: acquire and develop the hilltops.

By the early 1920s, some 70 parks, playgrounds, and scenic squares had been established, some obtained through individual benevolence. Designs for improvements were drawn up, and progress went ahead at a fair pace until the Great Depression, when the skilled construction laborers and strong young men who might have made the recreational projects a reality were laid off work. The city's dream came to a screeching halt. Then in 1933, during the first 100 days of

President Franklin Roosevelt's New Deal, several relief agencies were created to rehire workers and give the country a facelift at the same time. The Public Works Administration directly funded contractors to initiate needed construction jobs, such as the impressive retaining walls and stairways along Columbia Parkway.

Best known of these programs was the WPA, whose primary purpose it was to fund small local projects using simple construction techniques and local independent workers. Cincinnati city fathers recognized the once-in-a-lifetime opportunity and jumped at the chance. Not only did the city desire the federal funds to rehire the laborers, the Park Board was poised with Kessler's park improvement plans in hand!

Almost half of the existing 135 Cincinnati park shelters, comfort stations, entrances, and steps were built by WPA workers between 1929 and 1943, their "signature" and the date of completion framed in cement. Stone stairways were laid along park trails, and it is said that these same men also constructed some neighborhood steps. Obvious examples of the workers' handiwork include various Mount Echo, Alms Park, and Ault Park structures as well as the stone steps leading away from Bellevue Park (now overgrown and deteriorating) and the old walls and steps at Playhouse in the Park. Concrete playground slides were set into the natural terrain in Fernbank Park, Alms Park, and Burnet Woods, the latter a double-dip variety.

At its peak, the WPA provided relief to a third of the nation's unemployed—more than three million people. (Cincinnati women —about a thousand tailors, or seamstresses as they were known then—received WPA funds to repair donated clothing and fashion garments out of new fabric donated by the city for the poor.)

The Civil Works Administration (CWA), which existed from November 1933 to the spring of 1934, provided four million jobs nationwide, primarily in the building of roads, sewers, and schools. The CWA handled recreation-related projects, such as swimming pools and playgrounds, bathhouses, boathouses, camps, fireplaces, trails, and lakes, and forestry programs, such as planting trees and cutting fire lanes. The Krohn Conservatory was built with CWA funds, as were several Cincinnati neighborhood park pools, recreation buildings, and steps leading to and fro; Norwood's Water Works Park was also built by the CWA. During that same period, the Public Works Administration built the Columbia Parkway viaduct across Martin Street, the Celestial Street bridge and the several adjacent Celestial Street stairways, and the **Main Street Steps** in Mount Auburn. Road widening and drainage in western Hamilton County was also under their jurisdiction.

The Cincinnati contingent of the Civilian Conservation Corps (CCC) was made up entirely of African-Americans who camped in Cincinnati's largest park, Mount Airy Forest. Shelters, comfort stations, and steps were built there by the CCC, whose workers also built the Twin Lakes concession stand at Eden Park, the Owl's Nest Park pavilion in O'Bryonville, and the comfort station in Mount Washington's Stanbery Park. The original encampment buildings now serve as a public assistance center in Mount Airy.

Much like the Peace Corps, these federally employed workers —white men and black men—worked together, and those in the CCC lived together. They performed useful work for their country and received relatively good pay. All the men benefited from the physical work, the good food, the outdoor life, and the medical care they received. More important, the programs benefited generations of Cincinnatians, leaving us with a legacy of attractive amenities that it is our great privilege to cherish and maintain.

Walk No. 9

4.0 (or 5.0) miles

Mount Harrison

THE ROLLER-COASTER STREETS of this astonishing route display several lively Price Hill neighborhoods originally founded as a direct result of the inclined-plane railway. Until 1870, the area was known as Storrs Township. Our grand tour begins at the 8th Street bridge, intersects Warsaw Avenue, and continues on to exhibit the twin peaks where Swiss-descent Cincinnati pioneers Peter and Isabella Neff and their sons Peter Rudolf Neff and William Howard Neff once resided. From these historic spots, our tour proceeds into the Village of Warsaw. Nine interesting sets of steps are traversed.

For a five-mile hike, park on West 8th Street near the 8th Street bridge, heeding the rush hour signs, or park on Wells Street. Park on Warsaw Avenue near Del Monte Place if you favor a four-mile hike. The following directions begin with the longer walk.

· Descend the **Fairbanks Avenue Steps**; turn left on Fairbanks, then right on Price Avenue, and left on Woodlawn Avenue. Or, descend the **Woodlawn Avenue Steps** and proceed straight ahead.

· Turn right on Osage Avenue.

· Turn left on Mansion Avenue. Cross Kensington Place. These once-grand streets surrounded the former site of the Whittier Elementary School.

price's hills

- Proceed to Warsaw Avenue; turn right. If you opted for the shorter walk, your directions begin here.
- One block to Del Monte Avenue; cross, and enter the lovely long block of Del Monte Avenue; walk to Del Monte Place.
- Left of center, descend the bumpy blacktop-and-cinderblock **Del Monte Place Steps** to Brevier Avenue; turn right.
- As you continue along Brevier, the square-block park on your left (with beautiful steps facing Glenway Avenue) is Glenway Park.
- Right on Considine Avenue to Warsaw Avenue; turn left.
- Five short blocks down Warsaw to lovely Kingston Place; turn left.
- On the right, at the corner of Kingston and Stoddard Place, ascend the excellent **Kingston Place Steps** to Ring Place.
- Here is the site of the 40-acre William Howard Neff estate, which once sat alone on this apex. Turn right to take in a surprise overlook at the end of the lane.
- Turn around and follow the congested Ring Place to Grand Avenue; turn right.

- Right on Glenway Avenue. Stairways into the private Cincinnati Bible College and Seminary property—the site of the Peter Neff estate—are spectacular and can be viewed by continuing down Glenway one more block, before turning onto Wing Street.
- Left on Wing Street to ascend the few **Wing Street Steps** to Lehman Avenue. You are now scaling Mount Harrison.
- Left on Lehman Avenue five blocks, to Elberon Avenue; turn left.
- Right on Glenway for about six blocks.
- Right on the painstakingly restored **Wessels Avenue Steps**, going down the full block. Veer right on Wessels Lane to Carson Avenue. Sharp turn, where the cute little **Carson Avenue Steps** lead you to Mayfield Avenue and Park; turn left.
- Left on Ross Avenue. Cross Glenway, staying on red-brick lined Ross Avenue, passing stately old yellow-brick apartment buildings.
- Left on La Clede Avenue. Cross Carson Avenue, passing behind the Saint Lawrence church and school grounds. Cross

price's hills

Strum Street. Moving along, you encounter the La Clede
Avenue Steps, which coincide with the elevated sidewalk.
- Right on McPherson Avenue for the steep block-climb back to
  Warsaw Avenue. If you chose the shorter (four-mile) walk,
  turn left on Warsaw and proceed to your parked car. For the
  longer walk, cross Warsaw at the light, proceeding one-half
  block further to Van Vey Street; turn right.
- The pretty Van Vey Street Steps lie straight ahead of you,
  hugged by a granite block wall, leading to Enright Avenue.
- Left on Enright; old Saint Joseph's Cemetery is on your right.
  Follow Enright to West 8th Street. Left on West 8th to your
  parked car.

A Tale of Two Mansions

At the turn of the century, two mansions sat on opposite high hills
in Storrs Township, separated by a glen and a creek. They were the
Neff family mansions, built with splendid workmanship and from
fine materials, including stones quarried from the creek bed itself.
Each home had an unrivalled view of the prospering city of Cincinnati. The hills are still there. The glen, now dry, is known as Glenway
Avenue. The mansions, sad to say, are no more.

Each home has a glittering history. Peter Neff and his wife Isabella
Freeman Neff came to Cincinnati from Switzerland in 1835. Neff established a wholesale hardware business on Pearl Street between
Race and Vine Streets, importing the finest cutlery for use in the city's
pork industry. Long before the Price Hill Incline opened up the area
to development, Neff decided to construct a mansion in the western
hills, atop what was then called Mount Harrison. (William Henry
Harrison's hunting lodge was located in the dense woods nearby.)

The structure was fashioned from stone, featuring 12-foot ceilings; huge, ornate wooden doors; arched windows; and a broad veranda on all sides. An underground tunnel was dug between the mansion and the nearby coach house. The residence took two years to complete and was named Mistletoe Heights.

About 30 years later, Peter Neff and his sons, who were now also involved in the business, built a second mansion. Situated on the hill across the glen, this mansion was eventually occupied by eldest son William Howard Neff and his family. All members of the Neff family held deeply religious convictions and were active members of the community. William Howard and his father were among the founders of the incomparable Spring Grove Cemetery. The first interment in the new cemetery was that of Isabella Freeman Neff. When she died, her body was temporarily placed in the mausoleum of Judge Jacob Burnet in an old cemetery located where Washington Park is today, until the new burial ground at Spring Grove was opened.

Eventually, the William Howard Neff family branched off and moved elsewhere. Parcels of the 40-acre estate were sold off, and homes were attached to the hillside surrounding Ring Place, where the mansion stood. During the spring of 1944, a landslide caused the foundation of the home to sink, which resulted in the collapse of a section of the house. The home was condemned and razed a few weeks later.

In the meantime, Mistletoe Heights was inherited by another of Peter Neff's sons, Peter Rudolph, who was a child prodigy admitted to Woodward High School at age 10 years. Peter Rudolph was schooled in Greek, Latin, and French, in addition to the basic subjects, and he had a special flair for music and the arts. He served in the Union forces during the Civil War and rose to the rank of colonel. When he returned to Mistletoe Heights, it was to stay, as a family man himself. In 1878, Peter Rudolph, along with George Ward Nichols and Reuben Springer, cofounded the College of Music. Neff served as treasurer and later became president. He also served as president of the Philharmonic Orchestra and was involved in the Cincinnati May Festival. On October 1, 1883, Neff organized and founded the Westminster Presbyterian Church in the Mistletoe Heights front parlor.

In 1901, with his own children settling elsewhere, Peter Rudolph sold the estate to Dr. Brooks Beebe, who transformed it into the Grandview Sanitarium for the "care of cases of mental and nervous disorders, and the alcohol and drug habits." Peter Rudolph served as business manager of the sanitarium until 1910, when he went to live with one of his daughters in Chicago; he died there two years later.

In 1939, the sanitarium was purchased by the Cincinnati Bible College and Seminary. For 55 more years, Mistletoe Heights sur-

vived. The community seemed content, knowing that the religious Neff family would probably approve the estate now housing a seminary. But beginning in late 1995, rumors began to circulate that seminary administrators wanted to raze the mansion in favor of a chapel to be built on the site. The newly formed Price Hill Historical Society (PHHS) sprang into action, creating the Neff Mansion Preservation Association, an information and fund-raising campaign spearheaded by member Rob Geiger. The PHHS members offered various proposals and suggestions for saving the structure, but they were immediately made aware that the seminary administrators did not share their appreciation of the community's heritage.

The Mistletoe Mansion was one of the last remaining grande dames in the western hills. The Price family homes had disappeared; bootlegger George Remus's magnificent home and Grecian swimming pool on Hermosa Avenue and Eugenie Werk's Italian castle at Harrison and LaFeuille Avenues were likewise gone with the wind. Because plans for the chapel were scheduled "within the next few years," the members of the PHHS believed that they had time to spur interest in the project and raise funds. They garnered support from civic and historic groups and individuals throughout East and West Price Hills. They devised a plan to move the mansion to Glenway Park on Glenway Avenue between Purcell and Considine Avenues. There it would become a Town Hall, with meeting rooms and offices for various groups, and a historical museum. It would be a showcase for environment-friendly renovation and reuse, sublimely living up to the PHHS's goal of: "Preserving Yesterday, Today, for

Tomorrow." Utility companies were consulted regarding the viability of moving poles and wires in the mansion's path. House movers were contacted for their exorbitant estimates. Meetings between the PHHS and the seminary were not exactly discouraging, but seminary administrators would not commit to a promise to hold off demolition until funds to move the home could be raised.

At the conclusion of one such meeting in spring 1996, PHHS members were left with the impression that the situation was improving. To their horror, the stone coach house was pulled to the ground the very next day.

By summer 1997, the PHHS conceded that the mansion could not travel the distance to the chosen site. Still optimistic, members sought to purchase a site adjacent to the property. Although this solution seemed possible, it proved difficult to achieve. Time was of the essence. The campaign swung into full gear; pamphlets were circulated, and the media offered cooperation. Funding was available, but to get the money the PHHS had to submit a proposal detailing where the building would be located and how it would be maintained in the future. The August 1997 issue of the monthly PHHS newsletter, boasting of letters of support from all over the country, was mailed to members. But it was too late. Mistletoe Heights had been reduced to rubble on July 28, 1997. As television cameras recorded the historic mansion's final moments, the smiles gleaming on the faces of the seminary supporters appeared in stark contrast to the tears streaming down the faces of PHHS members.

price's hills

FAIRMOUNT

A S WE STOOD looking from the overview onto the downtown
skyline one person commented: This is a million-dollar
view. And I thought, surely this is why steps were created, to take
us to such beautiful places. Steps have existed for centuries and
created so many dreams. Thank "God" for the people who built
them, and those who lead us to them. When you climb steps like
these, and get to the top, it's like you were brought to this certain
point in time for a reason.

Ernie B. Smith; correspondence to author,
upon the opening of the Saint Clair Heights Park Steps

Walk No. 10

1.7 miles

North Fairmount (Shooter's Hill)

IN THE MID-1800S, Fairmount was a single community located atop and on either side of one of the steepest hills in Cincinnati. A grand and ornate Baptist seminary, a five-story affair with observation tower and two-deck terrace, overlooked the homes. This structure was used as a military academy during the Civil War, later becoming a medical college. In 1866, it was taken over by a German target-shooting society whose members labeled the entire domain *Schuetzenbuckel*, or "shooter's hill." The former seminary then became a resort of sorts, but it was never as popular as other Cincinnati fun spots because it had no incline to bring revelers to its heights. By any route, the walk up the fair mounts was steep and exhausting. In 1888, the resort, now a rundown boarding house, burned to the ground. Around the same time, the 18-acre park received the name Saint Clair Heights after General Arthur Saint Clair, the first Governor of the Northwest Territory. New steps climbed from Beekman Street to Fairmount Avenue; it is ironic that these steps that once served to link the residents on either side of the hill now symbolically divide the community into South Fairmount and North Fairmount. Nevertheless, Fairmount's history remains as one. As a result of neglect and redundancy, only about half the original 50 or so staircases remain open; the three or four choices visited in this walk are impressive, entertaining, and highly functional.

Park your car on Beekman between Dempsey and Baltimore.

- Walk west on Beekman, and right onto Fairmount. Walk to the end of this short block to find steps peeking out behind trees. Begin your ascent of the **Saint Clair Heights Park**

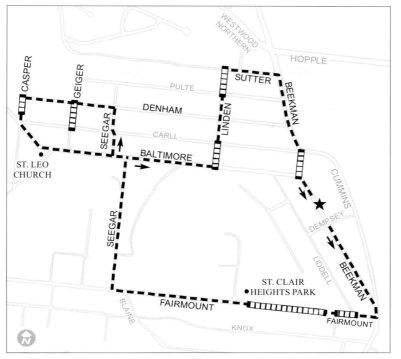

Steps, without a railing. The first set of these magnificent steps empties into an alley. Continue straight up the asphalt alley to its end. Locate the second set of steps and resume your climb. In the 1990s, after being closed for ten years, these steps previously known as the **Fairmount Avenue Steps** were restored and reopened. No other walk contains so many of these tri-step, precast stairs, positioned like notes along a long bar of music. The beautiful tree-canopied trail, nicknamed "the tunnel" by local residents, elevates 240 feet, which is equivalent to walking up 20 stories. Pause for a view at the top. Continue through Saint Clair Heights Park, much of which was lovingly restored by community volunteers with the help of community grants.

- Walk west on Fairmount Avenue for about four blocks. Turn right on Seegar Avenue for several blocks, staying to the right along the sidewalk. At the bottom of Seegar, turn left and walk a short distance north to the offset, continuation of Seegar. Cross Baltimore Avenue and continue down Seegar Avenue.

- Follow Seegar to Denham Street. Go left on Denham—no sidewalks. Stay on the west side of the street. You will encounter the **Geiger Street Steps** but, due to their deteriorated condition, pass them up and continue on to the end of Denham Street and descend the **Casper Street Steps**.

- Turn left onto Baltimore Avenue. On the right is the St. Leo The Great Catholic Church founded by German immigrants over one hundred years ago. Burundian, Congolese, and Guatemalan immigrants now call it home.
- Continue south on Baltimore for several blocks. At 1640 Baltimore, look carefully for the beautiful **Linden Street Steps** (no street, just steps), once cleaned by Bosnian, Vietnamese, and Cambodian working-welfare families during the summer of 1997. Descend the **Linden Street Steps** to Carll Street, continue on Linden Street to Pulte Street (about two blocks) to ascend another set of **Linden Street Steps** to Sutter Avenue.
- Turn right on Sutter Avenue to Beekman Street. Go right (south) on Beekman. Continue about three blocks, crossing at the traffic light. Ascend the well-maintained **Beekman**

fairmount

Street Steps, a set on each side of the road, complete with sturdy railings.

- Return to your parked car.

Annie Oakley

Odds are Phoebe Anne Oakley Mozee (Mosey) walked the old steps to *Schuetzenbuckel* Lodge atop the rural Saint Clair Heights Park on Thanksgiving Day in 1875. Even then, it was the fastest way to ascend "Shooter's Hill," where it is said she met and bested the famous shooter Frank Butler. Perhaps it was also love at first sight. Annie was 15 years old at the time; Butler was 25.

Born in North Star, Ohio, Mosey had traveled to Fairmount in Cincinnati to visit her sister Lydia (Mrs. Joseph Stein). Butler was visiting the city that November, for a one-night booking, appearing at the Coliseum Theater on Vine Street in Over-the-Rhine. He made a $100 wager that no one would outshoot him in the Fairmount park exhibition. Annie did.

Annie Mosey was number six of her Quaker parents' eight children. She was only five years old when her father died. The family lived together in a one-room log cabin with a sleeping loft. Annie, who loved being outdoors, began building traps to catch small game, providing meat for the table. A few years later, she learned to fire her father's long-unused muzzle-loading rifle, which was taller than she. Her aim was perfect. Her eyesight, reflexes, and coordination made her a dead-on sharpshooter, and soon their table had a surplus of game. The enterprising Mosey made an arrangement with a Greenville, Ohio, merchant. She cleaned, dressed, and neatly packed the game in swamp grass and shipped the box by stage to Greenville, where the birds were resold to the Bevis Hotel at Court and Walnut Streets in Cincinnati. The birds garnered top dollar. Annie shot them cleanly in the head, leaving no pellets in the flesh that might break a patron's tooth.

Less than a year after their Cincinnati meeting, Annie and Frank married. Shortly after that Frank's partner in the sideshow act became ill, and Annie Butler very capably replaced him, changing her name to Annie Oakley. For the next ten years, Butler and Oakley performed throughout the Midwest and a few major cities elsewhere. In 1884, while they were in New Orleans working with the Seals Brothers Circus, they spoke with Buffalo Bill Cody's agent about joining Cody's "Rocky Mountain and Prairie Exhibition," the hottest outdoor wild west show in the circuit. Cody already had a "family" act, but he invited the couple to try out in Louisville a year later.

The Butlers spent that time sharpening their skills and adding exciting theatrics to their act. On the first day in Louisville, they were hired on the spot. From 1885 to 1901 they toured with Buffalo Bill in summers, spending the winters on the North Star farm. (Cincinnati was a regular stop on the tour.) Oakley's accuracy with any kind of firearm became legendary. She could hit standing and flying targets one after the other and never miss. With her agile five-foot, 100-pound frame, she gracefully ran while blasting away with a gun in each hand, jumped over a table, picked up a couple of rifles, and continued blasting away before the target hit the ground. She shot from behind using a mirror. She shot while riding a horse. There was no fakery in the act, as was the case in some instances. Soon the small woman in the buckskin coat, short skirt, and cowgirl hat was stealing the show from Frank Butler and Buffalo Bill Cody but never-you-mind. "Wild West" eventually performed in 14 countries; on a tour of Europe, Oakley shot a cigarette from the lips of Kaiser Wilhelm II. (Later on it was said the Allies wished that, for once, she had missed.)

In October 1901, the train making the final stop of its tour crashed in Lexington, North Carolina. Four people died, 100 were injured, and 110 horses perished. Annie suffered back injuries that left her partially paralyzed. Told by doctors that her performing days were over, she fought back and recovered. Within two years she gave exhibitions and lessons while breaking her own records. During these years, Annie Oakley was generous to the poor, and having no children of her own, put 18 orphan girls through school.

In October 1922, the couple moved to the warmer climate of the south to benefit Annie's anemia. One month later, she suffered injuries in an automobile accident. In spite of a steel brace on her leg, she resumed her career. But the anemia worsened, and in 1926 the Butlers returned to Ohio. On November 3, 1926, Annie Oakley died in her sleep in Greenville. Nineteen days later, Frank, who was himself in bad health and living with his sister in Michigan, died. Both had given orders that their bodies be cremated, and on Thanksgiving Day, they were laid to rest side by side in a cemetery near Brock, Ohio, 12 miles north of Greenville.

Walk No. 11

2.0 miles

South Fairmount

THE HOPPLE STREET VIADUCT (1916), by which you may enter North Fairmount from Clifton, University Heights, Camp Washington, and Fairview, can be crossed on foot. So can the double-decker Western Hills Viaduct (1933), which at one time offered several sets of **Western Hills Viaduct Steps** from Central Avenue, Spring Grove Avenue, and State Avenue, accessing South Fairmount. Now only the steps to State Avenue are open. Originally, streetcars and trucks commanded the lower level of this viaduct, and pedestrians and automobiles used the top. From these bridges, the city views are vivacious. By connecting one or both of these viaducts with the Fairmount expedition, the dauntless walker earns extra miles of stimulating sights and sounds. This North Fairmount walk exhibits several other old staircases, giving a genuine perspective of an area once dominated by breweries and industry, yet always home to friendly working folks.

Park your car on Queen City Avenue near Quebec Road.

· On the northeast corner of Queen City and Quebec, take in the grand view of the old St. Francis Hospital. Built in 1888 on an abandoned cemetery, it was the only hospital west of the Alleghenies at that time to treat cancer patients. Closed as a hospital in 1981, it now operates as the Fairmount Senior Center.

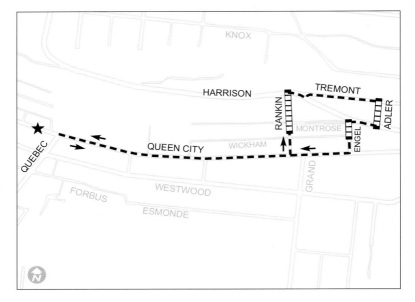

- Walk east on the sidewalk of Queen City Avenue about four blocks to Rankin Street. Turn left (north) on Rankin, and begin your walk up its steps and walkways. Cross over Montrose and continue to Harrison Avenue. The **Rankin Street Steps** still serve as a vital connection for bus riders of Route 21 on Harrison or of Route 6 on Queen City.
- Cross over Harrison, and go right, walking downhill about one block to Tremont Street. Enter Tremont, and walk east. Just past an abandoned lot are the now closed **Blaine Avenue Steps,** which at one time were much used by the residents of the Fairmont Hill neighborhoods. (I [Connie J. Harrell] lived on Tremont during my elementary school days, and

walked up these steps to the homes of my girlfriends farther up the Fairmont Hill.)

- Continue along Tremont to the Fairmount Methodist Church built in 1887. Cross over to access the lower section of the **Adler Street Steps** alongside the church. These obvious and lengthy staircases were named after Bernard Adler, who owned a woolen mill down on Harrison Avenue. Continue to Harrison.
- Right on Harrison for half a block; cross Harrison.
- Descend the **Engel Place Steps** to Wickham Place.
- Walk around to the front of the 1936 "modernistic" Western Hills Pumping Station of the Cincinnati Water Works; above each façade window is a metal panel showing an Egyptian water carrier. Before the property was fenced (sometime in the late 1960s), the waterworks hillside was perfect for sledding after a big snow.
- Cross Queen City and walk right (west) along its sidewalk, passing the South Fairmount Playground to your parked car.

The Legends of Bald Knob Mountain

Although Cincinnati's topography is compared with Rome's seven hills, the actual number of hills and mounts may be closer to four times that amount. Although many hills lost their distinctive nomenclature through the passage of time, such as Rose Hill in Avondale and Mount Harrison in Price Hill, one hill has had the dubious distinction of being given several names. The first name, often given to any cleared bluff in the United States from which it was believed that Indians spied on settlers or sent smoke signals, was Bald Knob

Mountain. Bald Hill and just plain Bald Knob are other names that appear in Cincinnati's early annals.

Whatever the name, it was never described as beautiful. In contrast to the lush greenery found elsewhere on Cincinnati's hills, bluffs, and valleys, Bald Knob Mountain was a barren, ugly spot. Some compared it with a denuded Sphinx; others nicknamed it Pancake Mountain.

However unlovely, in 1929 all eyes turned to Bald Knob. Because clay and dirt were needed to fill in the decaying Lincoln Park lake site where a railroad terminal and track yards were being proposed, the decision was made to dynamite Bald Knob and transport the loosened "spoil," dirt and rock fill, to the site of the future Union Terminal and Lincoln Park Drive (renamed for Cincinnati boxing legend, Ezzard Charles, in 1976).

The subsequent geological aberration resulted in "miraculous" sightings of the face of none other than Abraham Lincoln; some said his reclining silhouette was clearly outlined in the remaining knob. Others merely saw a cream puff.

Perhaps inspired (or provoked) by the carving of Mount Rushmore that had recently begun in South Dakota, *Cincinnati Post* reporter Eugene Segal had a public relations brainstorm. Why not use the Cincinnati hills for massive sculpturing projects? For example, how about carving Dracula into one of the city's many hillsides? Or Al Smith, Admiral Dewey, or Carrie Nation? Maybe Jimmy "Schnozzle" Durante?

Development, not massive sculpturing, ensued. During the following decades, the old Lehman homestead, located about halfway down Bald Knob, gave way to modest homes, skyrise apartments, and expansion of the Cincinnati Bible College and Seminary. The resulting landslides became legendary. In the 1970s, Bald Knob was further flattened to fill in parts of I-75. By this time, it was apparent that the entire hill needed to be reinforced.

Enter Will Radcliff, founder of the Slush Puppie Corporation. In 1980, Radcliff purchased Bald Knob, brought in clay to widen Lehman Road, restructured the bluff, and planted grass and shrubs. He built a road along the top of the bluff (which has a spectacular city view) and named it after himself. Although the resulting industrial park was affectionately named Nob Hill, another name was inevitable: Mount Slushmore.

fairmount

OVER-THE-RHINE

Pockets in the hillsides are largely settled by an overflow of inhabitants of the Over-the-Rhine area. . . . On the street level, each house juts up straight from the sidewalk. Many of the front windowsills support boxes of petunias. To one side there is usually a doorless hallway leading under the second story to a series of frame side porches, with steps zigzagging up from porch to porch. In the rear is the precipitous backyard, in which flowers and vegetables are often grown. Steep streets lead part way up the hillsides to these communities, but the principal means of access are the flights of wooden and concrete steps pressed against the slopes. On market days (at Findlay Market) women with huge baskets on their arms go down to the basin early in the morning and come back slowly up these steps, setting down their heavy baskets and shopping bags every few flights to catch their breath.

The WPA Guide to Cincinnati *(1943)*

Walk No. 12

2.2 miles

Findlay Market to Bellevue Hill

THIS LIVELY URBAN trek is a perfect example of Cincinnati's social intercourse: raucous in the Over-the-Rhine district and blissful in the Bellevue Park heights. There truly is no more memorable or definitive picture of life in old Cincinnati than that of the Findlay Market shopper descending the fabulous **Ohio Avenue Steps**, empty basket on arm, a couple of children in tow, heading for the sensual delights of Cincinnati's first "shopping mall." Returning home on steps or incline, laden with bags and string-tied parcels holding fresh catfish, skewered "city chickens," sauerkraut and spare ribs. Or perhaps a stewing chicken. Kale, leafy carrots, shiny red tomatoes, corn-on-the-cob. Morel mushrooms, black walnuts, juicy orchard fruits, rhubarb stalks, wild berries. Fresh eggs and butter from Russ Gibbs's dairy stand—a necessity. Luncheon meats and sausages to complement Ruebel's Rye Bread. Mustard pickles and sweet pearl onions. A bundt cake soaked in rum. Two bouquets of gladioli. And a brown paper bag of crisp but dumpling-like warm, salty pretzels. Most of these delicacies can still be purchased today. There was time then for conversation, rumor swapping, and bidding the seasonal greetings, and those activities still take place almost as unhurriedly as they did a century ago.

Named after James Findlay who owned the property and a prosperous log cabin store, it was originally an open-air market where

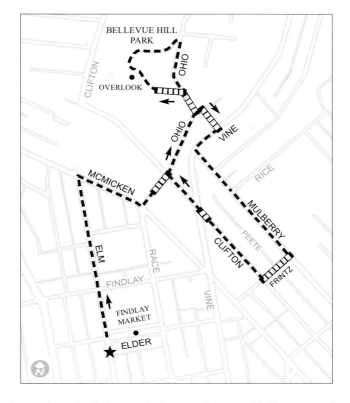

farmers brought their wares by horse and wagon. Findlay eventually became mayor of Cincinnati, and in the mid 1800s, he donated the site to the city. In turn, the city built an open-sided, cast-iron market building and began leasing stalls inside and out. In 1902, the house was enclosed and refrigeration was added. Throughout the decades, entrepreneurs of all types storefronted the square.

You can approach Findlay Market on foot from the Basin area. Elm (pronounced El-lum by some locals) Street guides you across Central Parkway, a handsome boulevard that replaced the Miami and Erie Canal, which had been drained and deepened for a subway system that was aborted during a scandalous 1920s political debacle. You will pass many other historic sites, including Music Hall and the Washington Park bandstand, and between 13th and 14th Streets, where the pavement has been peeled to reveal original trolley tracks and cobblestones. Enter the Findlay Market area in the next block, the first "suburb" annexed to Cincinnati.

For the driver, this walk begins in Findlay Market, where parking is readily available.

- Along the Elder sidewalk south of the market building, pause to read the interesting "anti-German Hysteria" plaque placed by the Ohio Historical Society and the University of Cincinnati.

- When you're ready to leave Findlay Market, walk north on Elm Street two blocks to McMicken Avenue to view the skimpy remains of the Bellevue Incline.
- Right on McMicken to Ohio Avenue.
- Just past (east) of the Philippus United Church of Christ, enter a cul-de-sac and climb the first of the **Ohio Avenue Steps**.
- Cross Clifton Avenue, and enter another section of Ohio Avenue. Walk one block past Kirk Alley to climb the remaining section of the lovely, scenic, historic **Ohio Avenue Steps** (on the left).
- Left at the pinnacle to climb the secretive 100, or so, stone **Bellevue Park Steps**. Or, if you'd rather take in pretty Ohio Avenue, move straight ahead to the park entrance.
- At the grand overlook, you will find the intriguing plaque honoring Dr. Daniel Ransohoff, professor at University of Cincinnati; the plaque also commemorates the Bellevue Incline and Bellevue House that sat on this lofty site.
- At this same spot, you can't help but notice the three mushroom-shaped concrete pergolas, each with a canopy of open grill-work supported by columns, designed by Carl Freund in the Frank Lloyd Wright style. The pergolas were supposed to be

over-the-rhine

covered with vines (and it sure would be nice if somebody
planted them).

- Return by way of the park road to Ohio Avenue.
- On Ohio, turn right and walk downhill to the end of Ohio Ave-
  nue. Descend the **Ohio Avenue Steps**, but at the alley turn
  left to descend the handsomely restored **Vine Street Steps**.
- Cross Vine Street. Turn left on
  Mulberry and walk east for two
  blocks to 97 Mulberry Street
  and the **Frintz Street Steps** (no
  street sign).
- Descend the **Frintz Street Steps** to
  Peete Street, and cross to continue the next set of **Frintz
  Street Steps** to Clifton Avenue.
- Cross to the south side of Clifton,
  and walk west on Clifton to
  Vine Street. Descend the few
  steps to Vine Street. Cross Vine
  to the west side of Clifton and
  continue to walk one short
  block to the **Ohio Avenue
  Steps**. Descend to the Philippus
  church, and walk to your
  parked car.

The Bellevue Incline

The Bellevue Inclined-Plane Railway, also called the Clifton, Elm
Street, or Ohio Avenue Incline, ran from the head of Elm Street at
McMicken Avenue to Ohio Avenue above. Built in 1876, its bottom
station officially proclaimed it "The Only Direct Route to Burnet
Woods Park, Zoological Garden and Clifton." It was 1000 slant-feet
long (give or take 20 or 30 feet depending on the source). At first,

the incline carried only foot passengers, but owners rebuilt it in 1890 to accommodate wagons and teams and streetcars. Situated next to the original McMicken Hall of the University of Cincinnati, the railway served commuters and students for 50 years.

Bellevue House, an imaginatively ornate roundhouse with a circular veranda audaciously cantilevered off the brow of Bellevue Hill, rejuvenated the incline travelers. It catered to the less discriminating, easy-going fun seeker who did not require art exhibits, sideshows (whales or otherwise), or any type of classical music. These mostly German-descent patrons enjoyed a traditional European beer garden similar to those in Over-the-Rhine, where singing and dancing to joyful live music and loud conversing were the priorities, next to beer, bratwursts, and sauerkraut. The panoramic view was a bonus. During the 1890s, no fewer than 113 festive establishments existed downtown between the river and McMillan Street, prompting some to refer to the region as "The Paris of America."

In 1901, fire destroyed Bellevue House. Although no one was injured, many cable cars burned. When the city did not include the Bellevue Incline in its 1926 plans for street transportation rehabilitation, the incline was closed and razed soon after.

CLIFTON HEIGHTS

THE SUDDEN TRANSITION from straight roadway to staggering flights of steps is an old habit with Cincinnati streets, an annoyance perhaps to the map-following motorist, but the typical gesture of defiance, the "never let a hill stop you" attitude of our streets and people.

Caroline Williams,
Cincinnati: Steeples, Streets, and Steps *(1962)*

Walk No. 13

2.2 miles

Fairview Hill

THIS WALK OF multiple lengthy staircases begins in Fairview Park, explores other fabulous Fairview strata, descends into Mohawk, and suddenly conquers Brighton Hill. The steps in this corner of town have a particularly unique history in that they served as commuter links for brewery workers, such as Bruckmann's, who labored throughout the day and night in Over-the-Rhine. At 800 feet above sea level and 300 feet above the admirably industrialized Mill Creek Valley, the heart of the city's economy, Fairview Park exists as a one-way, almost-mile long, horizontal slice in the hill called Scenic Drive. At any time of year, the view capacity is extravagant. From the western outlook, Mount Airy, Fairmount (including Bald Knob), and Price Hill seem to present a continuous ridge, part of what is known by geologists as the Cincinnati Arch. There is a glimpse of the Ohio River, with the Kentucky hills completing the encircling of Cincinnati's Basin. Union Terminal glistens like gold in the sunlight. Traffic on I-75 and Westwood–Northern Boulevard hums incessantly. The downtown outlook provides a rare "centered" view of the city.

Enter the park from McMillan Street (watch closely for it), near Clifton Heights. Park about halfway down Scenic Drive.

• Here you will spy the recently restored, comfortably designed **Warner Street Steps,** also known as the **Fairview Park Steps.**

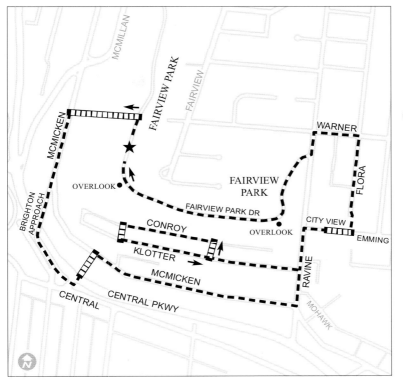

Descend these 200-plus risers, but before you do, turn around and locate the upper extension ruin of the original longer stairway. Torn out only a decade or so ago, those steps once allowed the climber to experience the actual path of the Fairview Incline, from McMicken Avenue to Fairview Heights, but, alas, no more. The closed upper extension of these steps going from Fairview Park Drive to Warner Street was known as the **Warner Street Steps**, a worthy extension of Warner Street above.

- At the bottom of the **Warner Street (Fairview Park) Steps** go left on McMicken for one block. Note the Brighton Approach sign, which is about all there is left to remind us of this historic community's roots. McMicken Avenue was once an Indian trail; from this pathway, General "Mad" Anthony Wayne's soldiers slaughtered Indians all the way into northwestern Ohio.

- Cross McMicken to the Brighton Approach. Continue down the approach staying to the left along the sidewalk. At the end of the approach you find yourself on an island once known as Brighton Corner—a transfer point for as many as six bus routes during the 1960s. This area once had many thriving businesses—two bridal shops, a clothing store, a quaint restaurant, a sporting goods store, and a bank.

- Walk to the traffic light on your left. Cross Central Parkway and walk up the **Brighton Place Steps**—which brings you back to McMicken Avenue.
- Turn right on McMicken. Before the neighborhood became the homes of young professionals, the **Kress, Baymiller,** and **Freeman Avenue Steps** linked the elevated hillside neighborhoods of Conroy Street and Klotter Avenue with McMicken Avenue. Multiple steps connected Conroy Street to Central Avenue, providing a walking connection from Fairview to Brighton and to the West End. These connections allowed access to several bus lines operating on McMicken, Central Parkway, and Bank. But, alas, those stairways have been either removed or gated, so you must continue along the McMicken sidewalk to Ravine Street. At McMicken and Ravine, there is a small park with memorials listing the neighborhood men and women who served and died in World War II.
- Left (north) on Ravine. From this location Mohawk Street can be observed. This was once a neighborhood of the same

name, where nasty Frances Trollope, mother of Anthony, lived and complained. This neighborhood was aptly described in the 1946 WPA Guide, "where small homes with side porches and outside stairways have been ingeniously constructed to suit the capricious slopes."

- Continue north on Ravine to go left on Klotter Avenue; you can see firsthand these beautifully redesigned homes.
- Watch for the quaint park steps on your right, just past 458 Klotter. Climb these steps to Conroy Street; again marvel at these multi-level homes on narrow lots with extraordinary views of the Ohio River Valley and Mill Creek Valley.
- Turn left on Conroy to another set of steps at 548 Conroy. Descend to Klotter.
- Turn left heading back towards Ravine. Take time to enjoy the Klotter views of the railroad yards and South Fairmount.
- At Ravine, cross the street and walk uphill (north) to City View Place.
- Right on City View Place to climb the steep **City View Place Steps**.
- Left on the elevated sidewalk to Flora Avenue.
- Left on Warner Street.
- Cross Ravine and walk downhill to the entrance to Fairview Park. Right onto Fairview Park Drive and enjoy the views at both overlooks as you walk to your car.
- Return to your parked car and exit onto Ravine Avenue.

The Fairview Incline

The Fairview Heights Inclined-Plane Railway was the last incline built in the city, at least 15 years after the other four, and the only one built by the City itself. It was the shortest incline at 700 slant-feet in length, 500 feet on solid rock and 200 feet on trestle at the top. It was the only incline to begin by hauling streetcars and end up with a stationary car for pedestrians.

The Fairview Incline's original purpose was to serve the No. 23 electric streetcar route that began at 4th and Central Streets, traveled through bustling Brighton by way of Colerain Avenue, and crossed a bridge over the Miami and Erie Canal to McMicken Avenue. At this point, it went up the incline and into Clifton Heights, down Fairview Avenue to Straight Street, to Clifton Avenue, and back again. The Harrison Avenue viaduct terminated at the bottom of the Fairview Incline at that time, bringing with it several streetcars coming from the western hills, so it began to be known as the Crosstown Incline.

The Fairview Incline was a serious, no-frills means of public transportation. No resort, no music, no beer or milk, no terraced overlook. As a Public Works endeavor, however, it arrived too late. By the turn of the century, it was obvious that roads for streetcars and automobiles would have to be built to accommodate the ever-expanding numbers of people traveling to and from the magnetic hillside suburbs. Ironically, as a means of transportation, the inclines had succeeded beyond wildest expectations, and by their success had greased the way for their own obsolescence.

As a novelty and attraction, however, they were always appreciated, long after they were gone.

Walk No. 14

1.6 (or 1.5) miles

Brighton Hill

THIS WALK OFFERS for exploration the steps off Central Parkway leading into the suburb once known as Brighton. No one seems to know for certain if the steps existed when Central Parkway was a waterway known as the Miami and Erie Canal, but they were surely trod by the butchers and tanners who worked at E. Kahn's & Sons, H. H. Meyers, and the Cincinnati Stockyards, when Brighton was the headquarters for the meat packing industry. Procter & Gamble sprouted up here before relocating to the Mill Creek Valley. Today, the lower neighborhood seems to be waking from a deep sleep, and if it weren't for the whirl of traffic on either side you might think you were out in the country. We continue on up the Brighton–Fairview hillsides via lengthy stairways, gently introducing the uninitiated to the treacherous delights of Straight Street and Ravine Street.

Unless you are familiar with this tiny Brighton community where the streets are narrow and isolated, you should park your car on McMicken Avenue near the **Warner Street Steps.**

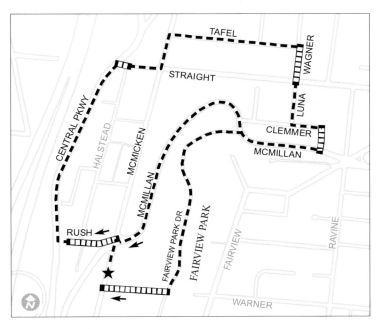

- Walk north on McMicken to cross McMillan Street. At the northwest corner of McMicken/McMillan, descend the **Rush Street Steps,** and follow the pathway at their bottom. At the end of the pathway, go right (north) along the Central Parkway sidewalk. Continue on Central Parkway for about two blocks to the **Straight Street Steps,** which begin behind a retaining wall. Walk up the **Straight Street Steps** to McMicken and cross.
- Left on McMicken, passing steep, steep Straight Street, to Tafel Street (which runs parallel to Straight Street).
- Right on Tafel; climb to the top.
- Right on the **Wagner Street Steps.**
- Cross Straight Street to enter Luna Avenue. (One block above, Straight Street is intersected by Ravine Street.)
- Left on Clemmer Avenue to the top; ascend the **Clemmer Avenue Steps.**
- Peek out on McMillan Avenue near the five-point intersection of the Clifton Heights shopping district. Hard-boiled detective writer Jonathan Valin once lived in and wrote about this notable neighborhood.
- Right on the busy, curvy McMillan Avenue for three long blocks. As you pass the entrance to Fairview Park, you are descending Brighton Hill. This crest was held hostage in the mid 1800s by a cluster of "Millerites," a cult believing the world would end on a specific date. When it didn't, leader William Miller designated a second date. When that doomsday likewise proved to be a dud, the disillusioned group did not return.
- If you would prefer to descend Brighton Hill on steps rather than on the McMillan sidewalk, cross McMillan and enter the Fairview Park drive. Proceed about a block into the park to the **Warner Street Steps (Fairview Park Steps)** on the

clifton heights

right. Descend these magnificent steps to your parked car on McMicken.

- Otherwise, if you descend the Brighton Hill on the McMillan sidewalk to McMicken, turn left on McMicken and walk south to your parked car.

Straight Street and Ravine Street

Straight Street was so named because it was the first thoroughfare to enter Clifton Heights from the Mill Creek in one bold climb, that is, straight up. Ravine Street seems to have been designated its opposite, inviting Heights dwellers to descend in a very speedy fashion! (Actually, the muddy path covered by Ravine Street's pavement was once indented, hence the name Ravine.) Although not as famous as San Francisco's trolley routes, these less-than-half-mile streets (plus a few others in Cincinnati) are comparable in perpendicularity, climbing about 25 feet per 100 feet horizontally and earning their reputations as two of Cincinnati's "baddest hills."

During the 1950s and 1960s, teenagers used these streets for a rite of passage; the driver would fly to the top of the hill, blinded by his or her own hood ornament, and career down to McMicken Avenue or Central Parkway without touching the brakes. Cars were heavier then. Traffic was friendlier. Teenagers were stupider.

Any way you do it—by Studebaker or on foot, bicycle, or roller blades—going up or down Straight Street or Ravine Street can be a first-class challenge. University of Cincinnati athletes do it. Bob Roncker, proprietor of the Running Spot in O'Bryonville, declares that many shoe purchasers boast of adding these hills to their lists

of accomplishments. Most infamous of the sports events, however, is the Straight Street Hill Climb. Sponsored by the Clifton Track Club, later known as the Running Club of Greater Cincinnati, the idea is to don summer running garb one early November morning, bring your Siberian husky if you have one, and gallop the 0.42-mile height as fast as possible. A sponsor of past events was Little Kings Ale, who provided six-packs at the top to toast in the holiday season. The King of the Hill usually made it in a little more than two minutes; the Queen took three minutes or more. In the mid-1990s, this race for pain lovers was voted the number one small race by readers of *Ohio Runner* magazine.

Winter on Straight Street and Ravine Street is a unique event; an icy rain or medium snow usually closes both streets down. Although they are two of the first streets salted and sanded (after expressways, ramps, bridges, and overpasses), mail is not delivered because walking (and sledding) can be even more dangerous than driving. Residents are captive (and without postal service) until city workers chemically treat strips, or ruts, in the snow and ice so that car tires and postal workers' boots can grasp pavement. If they were lucky enough to get out, residents return home by entering Straight or Ravine from a side street above their home address, slipping and sliding sideways while they attempt to rest their cars against the curb.

No doubt about it. Cincinnati is not a town for sissies.

clifton heights

THE WALNUT HILLS

B EHIND THE [Eden Park] Conservatory is a steep flight of steps. Adventure seems to be waiting at the top. There is a reward for those who make the climb; for here is the Eden Park Overlook, a high hill that looks over the Ohio River. The benches here always are filled with people watching the wonderful view of the river and the Kentucky hills beyond.

Mabel Morsbach, We Live in Cincinnati;
a publication of the Cincinnati Public Schools (1961)

Walk No. 15

4.5 (or 4.4) miles

Celebrity Tour

WALNUT HILLS IS steeped in history, layers upon layers of stories connected with the people who bumped elbows at the ever-changing, ever-bustling intersection of Gilbert and McMillan Avenues; this experience offers only a preamble. Several lengthy and different types of stairways exist around the perimeters of Walnut Hills—nineteenth-century viaduct steps, university steps, twentieth-century viaduct steps, and old park steps—each with its identifying ambiance. Within this walk, there is also a side excursion into an astonishing cul-de-sac overlooking the Ohio River. Upland Place contains homes so precious that the City of Cincinnati is in the process of qualifying the area for the National Register of Historic Places. However, not all the unique old homes are located here— quite the contrary. All along this route and elsewhere in Walnut Hills, homes and mansions that could not be duplicated today at any price stand proudly. Unfortunately, urban blight is likewise evident. Street names have historic significance: Kemper Lane is named for James Kemper, minister of Cincinnati's first church, whose squared-log cabin, the first home built in Cincinnati, was situated on what is now

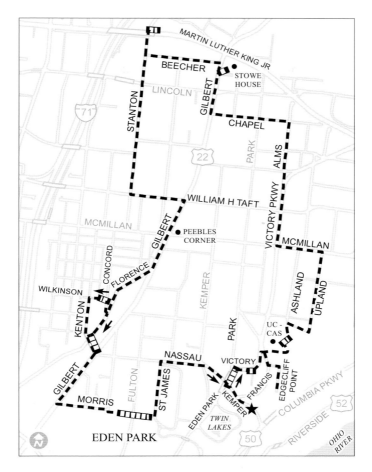

called Kemper Lane. Another minister who did not live in Cincinnati but whose influence was deeply felt was honored by another byway, the spacious Martin Luther King Drive.

Park on Kemper Lane, right or left side, off Columbia Parkway. The 11 flights of steps you are looking for to begin this walk are located just north of Francis Lane on the south side of the Victory Parkway Viaduct, which is over your head.

- The **Park Avenue Steps** are recently restored, regally marked, and a joy to ascend. At the top of the steps, at the viaduct where Eden Park Drive (or Park Drive, as it is known) becomes Victory Parkway, you continue straight ahead on Victory Parkway, toward the high-rise condominiums.
- Down a couple of steps at Calvin Cliff Lane. Continue walking on Victory Parkway. Turn right on Francis Lane, and cross the street. Turn left on Edgecliff Road, and then right on Edgecliff Point. Walk to the end of the road to take in the magnificent European-style villas, including Edgecliff Manor and the wonderful view from the cul-de-sac.

- Return to Victory Parkway, heading toward the University of Cincinnati, College of Applied Sciences campus. From 1935 to 1987, this site was occupied by Edgecliff Academy, an all-girls liberal arts school also known as Our Lady of Cincinnati College.
- Right at the red brick footpath curving around the administration building. Enter the terrace, and go down one of the two flights of **University of Cincinnati Steps** into the parking lot.
- Exit the parking lot at Upland Place (it looks like an alley) and head upward.
- Swing left at the corner of Upland Place and Upland Place, entering a paradise of fashionable Cincinnati homes that were built in the late nineteenth and early twentieth centuries.

    2206 is a half-timbered, half-brick building of exquisite taste, designed by local architect Lucian Plympton for his mother Cordelia, a decorator at the Rookwood Pottery.

    2214, also designed by Plympton, is the city's finest Swiss chalet.

    2300 is a knockout Victorian.

    2304 has a splendid coach house.

    2315 was built by Samuel Hannaford, a brick version of the Queen Anne style.

    2326 is known as chateauesque-style and is outstanding for its cone-roofed tower and diamond-patterned stonework; this home was once used as an art academy.

    2330 has great lightning rods.

    2334 is a lavish, Early Colonial style home, designed by another local architect, Fred Martens.
- Cross Fleming, continue to McMillan Street. On the right are three Saint Ursula Convent and Academy buildings. Before demolition for new construction, the Schuster-Martin School of Drama was located here; as a young man, actor Tyrone Power started acting classes there.

- Left on McMillan Street.
- Right on Victory Parkway, past the old Alms Hotel building.
- Veer left on Alms Place. Left on Chapel Street for three blocks. One of the stops on the Underground Railroad, this area boasted the first suburban Cincinnati African-American community.
- Right on Gilbert Avenue.
- At the corner of Gilbert and Foraker Avenues is Stowe House, where Lyman Beecher resided while he was president of Lane Seminary (1832–1849). With him at that time were two of his 11 children: Catharine, America's first domestic scientist, and Harriet, author of *Uncle Tom's Cabin*, who married Calvin Stowe, also a minister who became a seminary president. (Stowe house is open Tuesday, Wednesday, and Thursday from 10 A.M. until 4 P.M.)
- Cross Gilbert to continue along Beecher Street; 825 Beecher Street was the home of Wendell Phillips Dabney, author/editor of *Cincinnati's Colored Citizens* (1926).
- Left on Stanton Avenue. To your right are the several concrete viaduct **Martin Luther King Steps** should you wish to explore another day.
- Continue on Stanton for about five blocks; turn left on William Howard Taft Road.
- Right on Gilbert. When you reach Gilbert and McMillan, you are standing in the heart of historic Peebles (not People's) Corner, named after grocer Joseph Peebles who ordered international gourmet specialties for Cincinnatians for 50 years, until the Depression. Red-Hot Mama Sophie Tucker belted her tunes at the Orpheum Theater. At Greenwich Tavern, many an Irish tenor sang "Danny Boy" for his supper. Once-fabulous architecture can still be discerned.
- Left on Gilbert Avenue—once known as Gilbert Hill in this area—for about two blocks.

- Right on Florence Avenue for about two blocks. This area, adjacent to a spaghetti factory, was known as Little Italy.
- Right on Concord Avenue where you immediately spy the stone **Wilkinson Avenue Steps** on the west side. These steps lead to Kenton Avenue and then the Kenton Avenue Bridge, but, if you prefer a less circuitous route, continue down Florence to the **Florence Avenue–Kenton Street Bridge Steps**. Ascend the steps to Kenton Street. (There are other steps in the Kenton Street–Wilkinson Street area in various stages of picturesque decay.)
- Return to Gilbert Avenue. At this point you are standing about a block south of the "Walnut Hills" Bicentennial Commission historic marker that reveals the short, sensational history of the Gilbert Hill Cable Railway. Go back for a look.
- Cross Gilbert at the light and continue down to Morris Street; turn left. During the 1880s and 1890s, the grand stone building on your left housed the Eden School, founded by Blanche Fredin, wife of the French consul in Cincinnati.
- At the summit of Morris you will encounter the Beethoven Building. Follow the path in front of the building to the steps over the Eden Park hillside.
- Cross Fulton Avenue and continue up more **Eden Park Steps** and the pathway to Saint James Place.
- Left on Saint James; right on Nassau to Kemper Lane and your parked car.

For the more curious walkers and runners, the **McMillan Street Steps** at Reading Road add even more interest to this Walnut Hills tour. The Losantiville Triangle Park provides a good view of "Time" Hill: the Alpine-style building once housed the Gruen Watch Company, and the Tudor-style building once housed the Herschede Clock Company. The Stratford-upon-Avon building was once Beau Brummell Ties. Continuing on McMillan to Highland Avenue, the **Earnshaw Avenue Steps** behind Graeter's Ice Cream plant are certainly worth investigating.

The Boundary Line

It is no coincidence that Stowe House and the site of the earliest African-American settlement in Cincinnati are located in the same few blocks of Walnut Hills. It was from the Lane Theological Seminary, one of the final stops on the Underground Railway and one mile from the Ohio River Mason–Dixon Line, that many black men and women emerged from hiding to make a living on their own, free of the bonds of slavery. Not all Cincinnatians were sympathetic to the abolitionist cause, however; some estimate that half the city's residents favored returning slaves to the southern owners.

From Cincinnati, many black Americans went further north to Chicago or Canada. Others stayed and formed a social, intellectual, political, and financial nucleus of African-American culture around Lane Seminary, where they felt welcome. The Manse, a prominent all-black hotel, opened at 1004 Chapel Street; Wendell Phillips Dabney celebrated his 84th birthday there in 1949. Public schools for black children were accredited. Churches, groceries, law offices, beauty parlors, cigar stores, and saloons began to flourish. An African-American orphanage opened and moved to Avondale. Eventually, this network connected with other Midwest and eastern cities, including New York, and outgoing types traveled to meet other hospitable African-Americans.

One of the most well-known, respected, and loved black composers and musicians moving in this circle of celebrities was Wendell Phillips Dabney. Married to Nellie Foster, they resided on Beecher Street with their sons Leo and Maurice. Born in Richmond, Virginia, in November 1865, Dabney boasted that his life marked "the boundary line between American slavery and its present civilization." His father was a slave who bought his own freedom and became a wealthy caterer in Richmond, Virginia.

Dabney attended Oberlin College; he came to Cincinnati in 1894 to settle a relative's estate and settled himself as well. A year later, the Wurlitzer Company in Cincinnati published an instructional manual entitled "Standard Mandolin Method," written by Dabney and James Roach. Dabney also earned the position of head paymaster for the City of Cincinnati Treasury, a job he held for 21 years. Dabney wrote the music and lyrics for many songs. Sold as sheet music, they were mainly religious, but included the popular cowboy themes that he called "hillybilly" music. Although his accomplishments on the piano, guitar, mandolin, and banjo were described as masterful, he did not study music other than to train his ear.

At age 40, Dabney began publishing a weekly newspaper called the *Union*. Mostly a one-man show of news, opinion, and gossip, it was widely read and highly influential. Dabney's opinions on local and national racial prejudice were astute, witty, and sarcastic.

He maintained a second-floor office at 238 East 4th Street where he invited city visitors—black and sometimes white—to converse and perform and to meet others in the area who shared similar interests. Writers, artists, actors, musicians of all types, nuns, politicians, the poor, the rich—all converged in his office and home. In turn, Dabney frequently traveled to New York, Chicago, and elsewhere meeting and greeting the greats. He founded the Douglass League of Negro Republicans, but in time he became disenchanted with party politics in favor of voting for the individual.

One of the thousands inspired by Dabney was Cincinnatian Joseph Beaver, whose admiration for his friend began when he was 15 and Dabney was 72. Hired to assist with the paper, Beaver got to know Dabney intimately and well, and about 10 years later, he wrote a startling portrait of his mentor (brevity personified in 44 pages) simply entitled *I Want You to Know Wendell Phillips Dabney*. Beaver describes the handsome Dabney as an extraordinary and complicated self-made man, with an unquenchable zest for life. "He feared no man's slur," Beaver exclaims, detailing Dabney's abhorrence of violence while keeping a revolver lying on his desk.

In 1926, Dabney recognized the need to amass a local black history and published, from Dabney's Hall at 420 McAllister Street, documents, data, photos, and personal observations in *Cincinnati's Colored Citizens: Historical, Sociological, and Biographical*. Unusual for its time, the history included the contributions of not only male African-American movers and shakers, but also those of female entrepreneurs, maids, seamstresses, teachers, and philanthropists.

The slender, physically fit, six-foot-two Dabney wore a distinguished handlebar mustache. He exercised and often cooked his own homely but nutritious meals. He smoked an occasional cigar and drank an occasional Tom Collins "Senior." He quoted Shakespeare in his gruff voice, squirreled away rare books, and collected scrapbooks of art and interesting quotes that visitors could peruse. His office was hung with a few oil paintings and many photographs of friends, including W. C. Handy; Dr. W. E. B. DuBois; Luther/Bill "Bojangles" Robinson, who had also grown up in Richmond; Cincinnati educators Peter H. Clark and John Ison Gaines; poet Paul Lawrence Dunbar; and Charles P. Taft. In fact, the only copy of Beaver's biography in the Public Library of Cincinnati was copied from an autographed original that belonged to Charles P. Taft, until Beaver came to Cincinnati in 1970. Learning that the library did not have an original, Beaver donated one.

Around 1950, when Beaver visited Dabney for the last time, he found him still editing the *Union*. Dabney was 85 years old. Beaver described the encounter:

> His self-styled occupation is reading and writing with a few "breaks," producing a wealth in literary wisdom on events and ideas past and present, in an inimitable way in a veritable composite of brain, gift, and diligence culminating in the honest and bold expression of one man's opinion on whatever comes to his attention.

Some said Dabney's newspaper was constricted because it was all about Dabney's opinions. Others believed that it gave phenomenal insight into the "present civilization." Dabney died in June 1952. Having served 20 years with the U.S. Foreign Service in six countries, Joseph Beaver now resides in Palm Springs, California, where he is executive director of the African-American Society.

Walk No. 16

3.9 (or 4.0) miles

O'Bryonville to the Ohio River

THE HISTORY OF the steps in this eye-opening, stunningly picturesque walk reveals the once vital pedestrian links between the town of Pendleton—that portion of the East End directly below O'Bryonville—and the higher plateaus of Taft and Madison Roads. The area is one of majestic and modern mansions, a castle, two exclusive schools, and a quaint shopping district, and the scenery is spectacular in all seasons. The steps are still very much in use by walkers and runners. Most of the connecting steps from O'Bryonville down to the Ohio River have been closed or removed. However, remnants of these steps are evidence of the importance of foot travel before the automobile.

As you stroll, you may hear a church bell ringing nine times at 6:00 A.M., noon, and 6:00 P.M. That sound resonates from the largest swinging bell ever cast in the United States, belonging to Saint Francis DeSales Catholic Church at DeSales Corner (Madison and Woodburn). Nicknamed Big Joe and designed to compete with Big Ben, the bell rang but once, wreaking so much havoc on neighboring windows, structures, and ears that the gong was removed and replaced with a wooden side gong. (The original clapper may be viewed at the Verdin Bell and Clock Museum at 444 Reading Road).

Park on Madison Road, east of DeSales Corner, and near Cleinview Avenue.

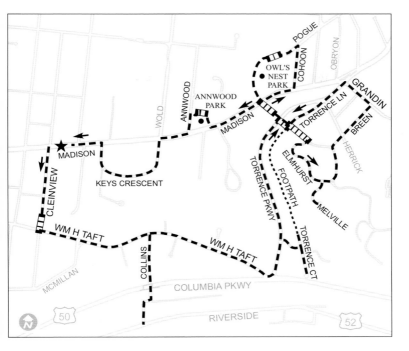

- Walk south on Cleinview Avenue, noting the Romanesque-structured, former Seventh Presbyterian church on the corner of Madison and Cleinview. At the end of Cleinview are the **Cleinview Avenue Steps.** This stairway leads to William Howard Taft Road.
- Turn left on Taft and walk east about three blocks. On the south side of Taft, watch for Collins Avenue which descends south to the Ohio River. If you want the exercise, walk the short distance (about 0.25 mile) down Collins to Riverside Drive and see the park along the Ohio River. You are at the bottom of the hill, the top of which is Madison Road where you parked. Retrace Collins Avenue back to Taft Road.
- At Taft, note, across the street where Collins would have continued north, the gravel-dirt road that serves as a driveway to private houses. This road leads to steps, known as the **Collins Avenue Steps,** which are now closed but in the past provided access to Keys Crescent Lane, which led to Madison Road. Prior to World War II, these steps were the main pedestrian walkway from O'Bryonville to the Ohio River area. The summit of these steps ends upon a private driveway, but this was part of the public route. Later in this walk, the top of these steps will be observed from Keys Crescent.
- Since we cannot access O'Bryonville up the **Collins Avenue Steps,** we will follow an alternate route. Continue east on Taft Road about 0.4 mile to Torrence Parkway. Cross Torrence, and walk north up its hill.

- The first street is Torrence Court. Walk up it to Torrence Lane, to the left of which is a bridle path, a gravel-dirt road. Continuing on Torrence Court, turn right and explore the cul-de-sac. Here you can see the Ohio River, and remnants of the Torrence Court Steps that led down to Columbia Parkway. Once providing access to the Pendleton Depot on the Little Miami commuter railroad, and to Saint Rose Parish, these steps were the last of the Columbia Parkway stairways to be closed. Return back on Torrence Court to the corner of Torrence Lane.

- There are two ways to proceed from this point. One choice is to take the Torrence Lane bridle path north. It borders the bottom of the large mansions on the right at the top of the hill. However, if the bridle path is muddy or too desolate, walk down the hill back to Torrence Parkway, then walk north on the sidewalk about three blocks to the Elmhurst Avenue Footbridge. Before going under the bridge, take the Elmhurst Avenue Steps to the right up to the corner of Elmhurst Avenue and Torrence Lane. If you walked on the bridle path, you would arrive at this same corner.

- Continue east on a second section of the Elmhurst Avenue Steps to the summit at the corner of Elmhurst Avenue and Elmhurst Place. Follow Elmhurst Place on the right, turning right on Melville Lane. Note the mansions overlooking the Ohio River, then return back to Elmhurst Place. Right on Elmhurst Place, taking in the spectacular cliffside scenery, circling left around the triangular flower bed; then back to Elmhurst Avenue.

- Right on Elmhurst Avenue; you will notice that it changes to Breen Street at the entrance of the Summit School for Boys, now Summit Country Day School for both sexes. Walk straight ahead on Breen to Grandin Road.

- Walk left on Grandin alongside another private school, the Springer School, to the stoplight at Torrence Parkway.
- Walk left on Torrence Parkway a short distance along the back of the Grandin House Apartments building to the next corner. Cross Herrick, and continue straight onto Torrence Lane to the left, rather than using the Torrence Parkway sidewalk to the right. Walk about one block to the corner of Torrence Lane and Elmhurst at the beginning of the bridle path.
- Turn right and take the Elmhurst Avenue Footbridge across Torrence Parkway to the third section of the excellently maintained **Elmhurst Avenue Staircase,** which is canopied by old catalpa trees that drop giant popcorn-like flowers in spring and long, skinny cigars in the autumn. These steps will take you to Madison Road.
- Turn right on Madison Road. You are at the west end of two blocks of specialty shops that make up the business district of O'Bryonville. Enjoy window-shopping as you walk to the stoplight at Madison and Torrence and O'Bryon.
- Cross Madison and return west along the shops on the north side of the street. Among the first-rate refreshments available in O'Bryonville are the irresistible delights of Bon-Bonerie, a bakery and café offering afternoon tea, breakfast, and lunch, as well as a bathroom. Continue for two blocks on the north side of Madison Road to Cohoon Street.
- Turn right onto Cohoon, and walk north to Pogue Avenue. Turn left and walk west on Pogue the short block to the entrance of Owl's Nest Park. Enter the park and follow the main sidewalk up the steps. Continue to follow the sidewalk to Madison Road. At the exit to Madison, note the park gates designed after those at Harvard Yard near the Charles River Bridge.

- Turn right and walk west on Madison Road for about two blocks to the first entrance sidewalk into Annwood Park. Follow this park sidewalk around to the very back of the park where it turns west, goes down a staircase, passes a large grotto, and takes you to Annwood Avenue. Turn left on Annwood Avenue and walk back to Madison Road.
- Turn right and walk one block west on Madison to the stoplight at Madison and Wold Avenue. Cross Madison at the light, and continue straight onto Keys Crescent. At the first curve to the right, look down the driveway of the first small house on the left, and observe the summit of the Collins Avenue Steps, now closed. These steps were the only steps in Cincinnati where the summit right-of-way was in use as a taxpayer's driveway. Earlier in the walk, we had commented on the lower entrance of these steps as we passed Taft and Collins. Follow Keys Crescent past the Holabird Luedeking House, Cincinnati's prettiest castle overlooking the Ohio River, and return to Madison.
- Turn left on Madison and walk to your car.

Saint Rose Church and the Pendleton Depot

While you're in the vicinity of O'Bryonville and its Pendleton (East End) counterpart, it would be well worth your time to visit Saint Rose Church on Eastern Avenue. The doors open on Saturday evening and Sunday morning for viewing what some consider the most beautiful old sanctuary in Cincinnati. You can't miss the steeple piercing the sky from the intersection of Torrence Parkway and Columbia Parkway.

Behind the church, there is a generous and close-up vista of the Ohio River. Downtown Dayton, Kentucky, sits opposite, showing off recently constructed, privately owned marinas. Turning around, you will see a measuring stick of all Ohio River floods from 1890

painted on the back of the 150-year-old building. (Flood stage is when the river rises above its pool stage of 52 feet.)

At the turn of the twentieth century, the towns of Pendleton and Fulton, further east, were home to German boatbuilders (see Walk No. 31). When architects drew up the blueprints for Saint Rose church, they proposed three clock faces for the sides of the steeple facing the shore, to benefit the local residents. Learning of the plans, Ohio River steamboat companies contacted the Catholic diocese of Cincinnati, offering to finance the fourth clock face that would front the river. Pocket timepieces were expensive in those days and often unreliable. River captains agreed that it would be good to have a point of reference on which to check their pocket watches as they approached the downtown public landing.

Pendleton was also connected with railroad travel. In front of the church, across Eastern Avenue, you can still see that Torrence Lane once intersected Columbia Parkway and served the contemporary and highly popular Little Miami commuter railroad. The ruins of the Pendleton Depot, named for George Pendleton, have been reclaimed by Mother Nature; so have the **Torrence Lane Steps**, east of the lane, that once led up to the station house. Additional signs of the Little Miami train-that-could (and still could today) are the ruins of nearly all 25 sets of stairs cutting through the retaining walls along both sides of Columbia Parkway between Wooster Pike and Torrence Road. Built in 1938 by the Public Works Administration, these stairs once served train passengers, and later bus passengers, until automobile traffic on Columbia Parkway swelled to a point too dangerous for any pedestrian traffic at all.

During the 1930s and 1940s, this area of Cincinnati was a bustling German-Irish community, socially linked to O'Bryonville. In fact, the pedestrian traffic back and forth over the various Elmhurst and Torrence steps were so popular with schoolchildren, workers, and shoppers that city engineers entertained the idea of an overpass across Columbia Parkway at Torrence. Produce markets at DeSales Corner and the butchers, bakers, and variety stores located at Peebles Corner attracted Pendeltonites. For O'Bryonville residents, the Collins Avenue Steps, now closed, were a quick shortcut to the Ohio River. East End high school students climbed the steps to Purcell on Hackberry, Saint Mary on Erie Avenue (later Marian on Madison Road), or Withrow, or just to Madison Road to catch the bus and eliminate or cut down on the three-bus-transfer route. Young men and women on both levels worked in grocery stores, five-and-ten-cent stores, variety stores, drugstores, gas stations, and restaurants; vied against each other on baseball and basketball teams; dated at movie theaters; and swilled tap beer in each other's saloons.

During the 1950s, after floods had weakened or taken many of their wood-frame residences, and chain stores and restaurants were destroying family businesses throughout the area, many old families departed Saint Rose Parish. When the diocese contemplated whether the riverfront church might prove too costly to maintain, Father Cornelius Jansen was assigned to see what he could do. Jansen, a highly intelligent, extremely industrious Dutchman, decided that the best way to save the church was to have it qualify for the National Register of Historic Places. Jansen had another asset: he gave a short sermon. Attracted by the 25-minute mass and the attention being given to the grand old church, well-to-do Catholics from the eastern hills and relocated parishioners began to fill the collection plates. As a result, the church was refurbished from the cross atop the steeple down to the bingo halls in the basement. Jansen himself fine-tuned the four clocks.

The rest is a matter of historic register. Saint Rose and Saint Francis DeSales Churches both qualified and remain vital to this day.

MOUNT LOOKOUT

STEPS WERE A big part of my life. And a pain in the neck. For years I walked from my house on Rushton Road to Cardinal Pacelli grade school over the **Ellison Avenue Steps,** with my friends Ronnie and David. Up the steps, down the steps. That was the price one paid for living on a Cincinnati hill. If I stayed after school for Blue Birds I'd have to walk by myself. Up the steps, down the steps. I dreaded it. I remember hearing noises and being scared, wondering why my mother allowed me to walk through the woods all by myself. In high school, I used what we called the "viaduct" steps. In the morning, I went down the viaduct steps from Grandin Road to Delta Avenue to catch the bus to Saint Mary, and then it was back up the steps after school. Sometimes I'd take my time; sometimes I'd see how quickly I could make it up or down. In the summer, there were wild hollyhocks, hundreds of them, along the viaduct steps. As children, my friend Margie, who lived next to the steps, and I climbed on the bottom of the viaduct, and in the winter rode our sleds from Grandin Road into her yard, climbed the steps, and rode down again. Now when I see the steps, they stir up happy memories from my childhood. But I still don't want to climb them. Actually, I don't think I could without taking a Coke break halfway up.

Suzanne Stratman Machenheimer,
former Mount Lookout resident

Walk No. 17

2.6 miles

Mount Lookout Square

According to *The WPA Guide to Cincinnati,* (1943 and 1987), the general description of Mount Lookout, Hyde Park, and East Walnut Hills, so intricately and domestically related, is that of residential neighborhoods reflecting "more-than-average prosperity." Time has not changed this assessment. As you walk along under old oaks and elms, you will encounter lucky residents of this spunky suburb; they are friendly and fun and always seem on the go. They love their children. They love their dogs. This formidable introductory walk begins and ends at steps within the boundaries but on opposite sides of Mount Lookout Square, making a somewhat rectangular pattern as you traipse the nearby peaks and valleys from one captivating point to another. Throughout the adventure you will notice European, British, and Mediterranean influences on the American architecture of these classy, manageable homes; homes perched atop private stairways reflecting more-than-average creativity in design and execution. Here too are some of the city's best flags and awnings. Although this hike is rather romantic at dusk 364 days a year, it is positively enchanting the one evening in December when Christmas luminarias grace yards, porches, paths, curbs, and steps.

Park somewhere in the middle of or along the street near Mount Lookout Square. Meters are in effect from 7:00 A.M. to 6:00 P.M.: 120 minutes in the square parking lot; 60 and 120 minutes for on-street parking.

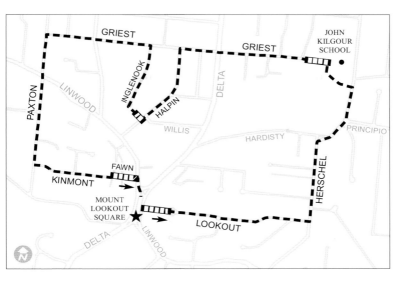

- Begin your journey at the wide, handrailed, earthy **Lookout Lane Steps** located on the east side of Delta Avenue, next to the Bracke Building. Turn around for the lookout at the top of this stairway.
- Move forward from Lookout Circle to Lookout Drive to Herschel Avenue.
- Left on Herschel for three blocks; go through the all-way stop at Hardisty Avenue, continuing on Herschel.
- Go to the right behind the John Kilgour School (1928), the land for which was donated and the school named by Mary Kilgour in memory of her beloved husband. Centrally located along the chain-link fence you will find a step-path from Herschel to Griest Avenue. This delightful ravine shortcut for children going to and coming from school, known as the **Griest Avenue Steps**, was laid many years ago. It should be used only when school is not in session; descend. If school is in session, pass the John Kilgour school and turn left on Suncrest Drive, proceeding around to Griest Avenue; turn right.

- Follow the ups and downs of Griest Avenue for about one-quarter mile. Cross Delta Avenue at the light.
- Left on Halpin Avenue for two long blocks (almost to Linwood Avenue). Watch for the **Inglenook Place Steps** just past Willis Avenue on the right.
- Ascend the **Inglenook Place Steps.** Walk north on Inglenook Place, and turn left on Griest.
- Travel all the way to Paxton Avenue where Griest dead-ends; the sidewalk dwindles along the last two blocks of Griest, but there is very little traffic here.
- Left on Paxton for one long block. Cross Linwood Avenue (once a toll road) at the light.
- Upward on Paxton about three blocks.
- The next turn you make is onto Kinmont Street, which intercepts Paxton at the knoll, not the peak. Left on Kinmont.

- Follow Kinmont (no sidewalk for about one-half block) until you catch sight of the lengthy and secluded **Fawn Alley Steps**.
- Descend to Mount Lookout Square and your parked car.

The Delta Avenue Connections

Once the pebbled bed of Crawfish Creek, Delta Avenue eventually became a handy shortcut between the rural village of Hyde Park and the "eastern avenue" leading into the city. Kilgour brothers Charles and John, who resided in Hyde Park, built a narrow-gauge railroad along Crawfish Creek to stimulate settlement and relieve transportation difficulties, including their own. John Kilgour was president of the Cincinnati Street Railway.

But it wasn't until the city annexed Hyde Park that population numbers soared, and the town of Mount Lookout, situated in the approximate center of what would eventually be known as Delta Avenue, came into existence. As people moved in, the traffic grew, and the railroad was supplanted by trolley, trolley bus, bus, and an ever-increasing stream of automobiles. Delta Avenue, widened and paved, served as the most vital north–south artery on the east side.

During the 1950s, Cincinnati Utilities Director George Howie, a controversial traffic controller, took action to sort out the dangerous chaos on Delta and Linwood Avenues by inserting stoplights and "Howie's hurdles" in the center of the square, creating 32 new parking spaces. Although he bore ridicule for his hurdles elsewhere, in Mount Lookout they led to an improved infrastructure and were a huge success. Celebrities joining the crowd who came to gawk at the town square reopening one night in October 1952 included City Manager W. R. Kellogg (for whom the pike was named), Uncle Al Lewis, Captain Wendy Lewis, and disc jockey Paul Dixon, who was a Mount Lookout resident. Howie attended; one would hope that he received a few accolades in his lifetime for helping Mount Lookout become the thriving town center it remains today, a place to see and be seen, rather than just another suburban byway.

Walk No. 18

3.5 miles

Around Ault Park

AULT PARK, CROWNING Mount Lookout, is the perfect setting for taking a walk at any time, but particularly at sunrise, sunset, and moonrise, when the view from the grand, columned observation pavilion—elevation 810 feet—is glorious. Here are the city's foremost formal steps, those leading up to the pavilion itself. Among the other fine staircases on this strenuous stroll are the stylish, gaslit steps leading to the Cincinnati Observatory. In between, you will enjoy a half-mile trek through Hyde Park East and have the opportunity to casually study the architecture and artful landscaping of stately, expensive homes built during every decade of the past 60 or so years. You will also want to take note of the aircraft arriving and departing Lunken Airport in the skies overhead: propeller planes, including vintage World War II planes; snazzy corporate jets; helicopters, private and military; and the ubiquitous blimp during sports events of national interest.

Park on Observatory Circle and climb the hill or the elegant, broad **Ault Park Steps** fronting the pavilion.

- Climb the pavilion steps to the rooftop promenade to enjoy this pastoral view. To the south, the water tower marks the crest of Mount Washington, with the just-visible Kentucky hills on the right. The extensive Little Miami River valley and its steep banks, including those of Indian Hill, carve a path through the hills to the east. To the north, the wooded hillside obstructs Madisonville, Oakley, and Norwood. To the west, downtown points of reference include Mount

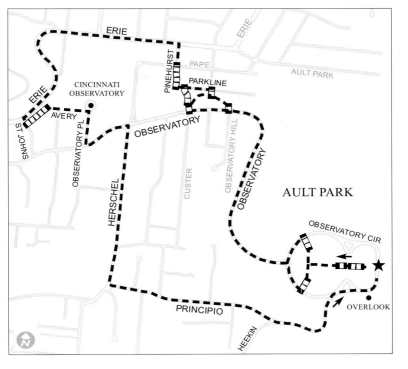

Adams, the Carew Tower, and the spire of Saint Francis DeSales church.

- Go down the pavilion steps, walking south to gasp at the worst un-hyphenated plaque ever bronzed, honoring Levi Ault, Cincinnati's first park board president (1900–1926). The park was named for Mr. and Mrs. Ault (she was spared the bronzed recognition), who donated 200 of the 235 acres for the site. If you walk to the north of the pavilion, you will see the Ault Park Rededication Monument erected in 1991. Listed on its four sides are the names of all those whose concern and generosity were instrumental in the efforts to restore this magnificent park.

- Descend the **Ault Park Steps,** two flights separated by the lovely art deco water cascade, progressing in a westerly direction into the lavishly planted quasi-formal gardens.

- Meander the garden paths, up and down the steps, as you desire.

- Exit by one of the stairways on the west side and proceed to Observatory Avenue; the sidewalk is on the left.

- Proceed down the Observatory Avenue ravine, and then up through the grove of Japanese weeping cherry trees that burst into a glittering pink haze of blossoms in early April.

- Cross at Observatory Hill to descend one of the three sets of handrailed **Parkline Avenue Steps** that spill out, Y-fashion, onto Parkline Avenue.

- Left on Parkline one block. (Note the primitive **Ault Park Steps** on the left leading back up to Observatory Avenue.)
- Descend the **Pinehurst Avenue Steps** and path to Pape Avenue.
- Straight ahead on Pinehurst Lane one block to Erie Avenue; turn left.
- Continue your half-mile stroll through Hyde Park East, crossing Marburg Avenue, veering around the bend.
- Left on Saint Johns Place. Immediately ascend the **Avery Lane Steps**—hollow cinder-block steps accented by gaslights, escalating to a long blacktop path—to the heroic Cincinnati Observatory (discussed in Walk No. 4). Pause to take in the sights.
- Right on Observatory Court.
- Left on Observatory Avenue, crossing Herschel, to proceed back into the park and to your parked car. (To lengthen your walk, turn right at Herschel and reenter the park via Principio Avenue.)

Located in the woods north of the pavilion is a ravine trail containing about 300 wood and stone steps, some of them limestone from the creek bed below. Because this forest is one of the least disturbed stands of old-growth trees in Cincinnati, Xavier University biologists have developed a half-mile-plus Tree Walk complete with map. Illustrative signs are in place off the service road, in the rear of the north parking lot, and near the cherry tree grove.

Dance Steps

Nationally recognized landscape artist A. D. Taylor designed the figure-eight layout of the drive and the formal gardens within Ault Park. He went on to a distinguished career with the National Park Service. Local architects Fechheimer and Ihorst designed the two-

deck pavilion with dancing in mind. Young people residing on the terraces of eastern Cincinnati held this same interest; indeed, dancing was the national pastime during the 1920s and 1930s, up until World War II. Couples had an astonishing number of popular dance steps in their 1930s repertoire: the Two-Step, the Black Bottom, the Apple Jack, the Big Apple, the Jitterbug, and, of course, the Waltz, played by various local and traveling orchestras, including the men- and women-musicians of Mr. Pink's Dance Band.

The Jimmy James Band, the Don Harmon rock-and-roll combo, and Charlie Kehrer played music in the park during the 1940s and 1950s. George "Smittie" Smith's band gave park concerts for 50 years until the early 1960s, when African-American Cincinnatians demanded their fair share of what had been up until then all-white frivolities. The park temporarily closed after the costly damage done during the racial protests. In time, new and enthusiastic benefactors restored beauty and pride, and by 1976, Ault Park was once again a center for leisure activities—for all.

The pavilion hosts wedding ceremonies and photographers on weekends in spring, summer, and fall, and an occasional dance band once again sets toes a-tapping. When the sun goes down, the artful lighting produces a romantic ambiance reminiscent of Brighton or Bournemouth, and the landscape is just as hypnotic as it was when our ancestors waltzed and wooed, and wished for undying love on first and falling stars.

Walk No. 19

2.9 miles

Grandin Road

THE FIRST AND most impressive set of steps on this merry march once accessed the mighty Grandin Road Viaduct, which used to connect the twin bluffs on either side of Delta Avenue (the bridge was razed in 1975). Consequently, we begin at the Grandin Road Gap and take in the hills and valleys on the east side of Delta Avenue and Grandin Road only, but do not despair. Mount Lookout leaves nothing to be desired. In the spring, talented gardeners generously display beds of iridescent phlox, lavish clumps of daffodils and jonquils, tulips of every color and size, showoff perennials and confident wildflowers, glowing azaleas and rhododendrons—all keeping beautiful company with waving tendrils of bright yellow forsythia, redbuds, pink and white dogwoods, spiky japonica, and decoratively shaped apple and pear trees.

Park on Delta Avenue, near Kroger Avenue.

- Ascend the 24 flights of **Grandin Road Steps**, four to six steps each, passing between Longworth Court condos to the north and lovely one-family homes to the south. Branches extending from honeysuckle bushes, mulberry trees, and resin-scented Douglas firs create a pleasant canopy overhead.
- When you reach the summit, pause to look around and imagine a huge, 100-foot-high bridge that joined both sides of

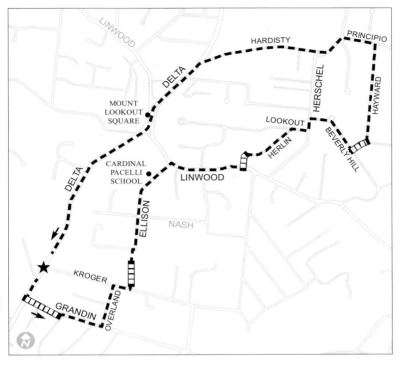

Grandin Road. Wouldn't it be nice if a mirror set of steps lead to Grandin Road west, thus rejoining Grandin Road (on foot, anyway) and connecting our Mount Lookout and O'Bryonville Walks?

- Continue up Grandin Road to Overland Avenue; turn left (no sidewalk).
- Right on Kroger Avenue about one-half block.
- Across the street, at 3600 Kroger, you will spy the entrance curvature of the **Ellison Avenue Steps** sitting back off the curb. This recently restored stairway peaks in the center; note the compact structure of the new step, offering a deeper tread and more space for the foot, thanks to an efficiently angled riser. As you descend, you will notice that you are in the vicinity of the Mount Lookout Swim Club, where, in the summer, you may admire the tan and fit bathers, some of whom use these steps to get there.

- Move ahead, along the Ellison Avenue ridge, crossing Totten Avenue and Nash Avenue.
- As you pass the Cardinal Pacelli School, you might wish to ascend the steps zigzagging up the well-preserved hillock to the school. Afterwards descend back to Ellison, continuing your walk towards Linwood Avenue.
- Cross Linwood; turn right.
- Travel two long blocks, watching for the **Herlin Lane Steps**, which have handrails on both sides. Take this agreeable step-path to the Herlin Place cul-de-sac.
- Right on Lookout Drive.
- Left on Herschel Avenue. Right on Beverly Hill Drive.
- About half a block along Beverly Hill you might discover the tidy footpath propelling you toward Linwood Avenue; no steps. Save this path for another day. Continue another half block to 1151 Beverly Hill Drive, where, across the street, you will find the **Beverly Hill Drive Steps**; ascend.
- Left on Hayward Avenue.

- Left on Principio Avenue. Left on Herschel Avenue to the triangle, then right on Hardisty Avenue.
- Left on Delta Avenue, heading south. It is eight-tenths of a mile from Mount Lookout Square to your parked car, a distance made especially agreeable because every dwelling on Delta Avenue is approached by lengthy, startlingly attractive, or just plain startling, sets of stairs, none of them exactly alike.

The Ill-Fated Viaduct

When the Grandin Road Viaduct was proposed at the turn of the twentieth century, wealthy East Walnut Hills and Tusculum Heights residents agreed to give the city the right of way free of charge. This benevolent attitude was a far cry from the prevailing sentiment when the viaduct came down 75 years later.

The original concept allowed streetcars to bridge the chasm so that these residents would not have to walk down the steep slope to

Delta Avenue for transportation. Also involved was the hope that the area would be improved by continued residential development. This hope flowered as investors eagerly took advantage of the opportunity to reside or put capital in land near Longworth's Rookwood mansion and the prestigious Cincinnati Golf and Country Club and to rub shoulders with neighbors such as the Emerys and LeBlonds. Not until this available acreage was exhausted did the town of Indian Hill come to be.

Private cars ended the rail usage, but the viaduct remained a handy commute and connection, and never more so than when the Ohio River flooded Eastern Avenue or traffic jammed Columbia Parkway. But there were problems. Shifting land and corrosion caused costly repairs, and would-be pranksters began a reign of strife. Among the items hurled onto Delta Avenue from the bridge, some 100 feet above, were pumpkins, liquor bottles, snowballs, bricks and rocks, bicycles, and firecracker bombs. Once, during the middle of the night, a cement park bench came crashing down; luckily no one was injured.

Locals nicknamed the viaduct Lover's Leap, claiming it attracted suicides. One particularly tragic story involved three friends, East End men, two of them brothers. Not particularly fond of book learning, the brothers decided to join the Armed Services rather than finish high school. The younger boy, a Marine stationed in the Philippines, was mysteriously shot and killed. The older, also the victim of a military accident, fell off his ship into Puget Sound. The third young man, their best friend—perhaps distraught with guilt for surviving while his friends had perished—climbed the steps and jumped to his death off the Grandin Road Viaduct. All three fellows, once full of life and expectation, died in the same year.

In April 1956, a socialite was murdered in her home on one of the lanes off Grandin Road (now considered Hyde Park, not east Walnut Hills). The meter reader who killed her used the Grandin Road Viaduct to make his escape, further tarnishing its reputation.

Rather than spend money on more repairs and safety renovations, the city elected to raze the bridge in 1975. Controversy still exists today about this decision; some believe that Grandin Road residents unfairly used their wealth and power to coerce the city into razing the bridge, thereby guarding their privacy and protecting their property from other (perhaps not so elite) Cincinnati residents who needed the viaduct.

ELBERON HEIGHTS

I CONSIDER MYSELF fortunate to have been involved in Cincinnati's City Hillside Stair Study. In doing the 1980 survey, I got to walk all of the city's steps (over 400 sets) and see all areas of the city. I discovered some interesting shortcuts between neighborhoods and met some fascinating people. Some of the steps seemed remote and isolated, where the only noises were from the squirrels and birds or the wind rustling the leaves. We (my partner Dick Hater and I) found it a great way to stay in shape.

Jim Mills,
City of Cincinnati Architectural Technician

Walk No. 20

3.7 miles

Overlook Avenue

THE WEST PRICE HILL walk occupies three distinct western hills neighborhoods. The historical perspective of this stroll is outstanding, and the steps and paths, not so few but far between, are excellent. The starting point is Western Hills High School, passing through three stairways that lovingly connect the vertical Prosperity Place cul-de-sacs. This is an area of closely situated homes with peaked roofs that somewhat resembles an Alpine village when the snow falls. From here we go left on Glenway Avenue, into the bustling Overlook shopping district, continuing on to south Overlook Avenue and the inspiration for the Spanish motif in the neighborhood: old Saint Teresa of Avila Catholic Church. Here we get a hint of the many outdoor treats the Price Hill Historical Society's premiere Holiday Home Tour includes. (Indoors, for example, tour-takers learn that Rookwood fireplaces are commonplace.) The end of this walk is especially pretty in the evening.

Park at or near Western Hills High School, which is on Ferguson Road near Glenway Avenue.

- Behind the school, follow the cement path, with steps, along the Cincinnati Recreation Department tennis courts, to the

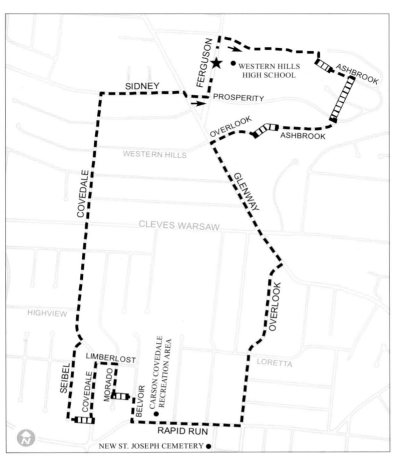

blacktop path, to the first set of **Ashbrook Drive Steps** at
the end.

- Walk down Ashbrook Drive about one-half block to the center-
  handrailed **Prosperity Place Steps** just past 1885 Ashbrook
  on the right. Cross Green Glen and ascend the next segment
  of the **Prosperity Place Steps**.
- Left on Prosperity; right on Ashbrook again to the awesome
  second set of **Ashbrook Drive Steps** at the cul-de-sac. Head
  up to North Overlook Avenue, then straight ahead.
- Left on Glenway Avenue for about three blocks, crossing Cleves
  Warsaw Pike.
- Right on Overlook Avenue. At the corner stand two historic
  Saint Teresa of Avila churches, the older, facing Overlook
  Avenue, is the photogenic Spanish Mission-style building,
  now a meeting hall. The new church and graceful bell tower,
  a neo-Romanesque style built in 1962, face Glenway Avenue.
- Follow Overlook Avenue for three long blocks, previewing a
  few of the aesthetic delights of the Home Tour, and enjoying

glimpses of the views behind the homes on the eastern side of Overlook, when available:

1124 displays the Prairie Box or American Foursquare home.

1121 is a Tudor Revival with half-timbered twin gables and the red tile roof that distinguishes this neighborhood.

1063 was one of the first homes built on Overlook Avenue, in 1914.

1026 defines the word "bungalow," with its horizontal lines, low-pitched roof, and ample front porch.

1021 is basically a Colonial Revival-style home, with red tile-hipped roof and eyebrow dormers. It stands on what was once the 10th green of the Elberon Golf Course.

- Right on Rapid Run Pike.
- Go three blocks on Rapid Run Pike, continuing alongside the New Saint Joseph Cemetery.
- Just past the Carson Covedale Recreation Area go right on the Belvoir Lane cement path, which leads to the cul-de-sac; left on the next path to the **Belvoir Lane Steps** to Morado Drive.
- Right on Morado Drive.
- Left on Limberlost Lane.
- Left on Covedale Avenue for one long block. Cross Covedale to ascend the **Covedale Avenue Steps** between homes, to Seibel Lane.
- Right on Seibel, back to Covedale.
- Left on Covedale for a lovely three-quarters of a mile walk to Sidney Road; turn right.
- At Glenway, jog on over to Prosperity Place, to Ferguson Road, to Western Hills High School and your parked car.

elberon heights

Prosperity Place

One of the first things any student of Cincinnati culture learns is that once the Basin and Over-the-Rhine were populated and polluted, citizens took to the hills, en masse. Conditions must have been awful if even the Cincinnati Observatory telescope developed a cataract. Fear of disease, such as "ague" (chills and fever) and cholera, and malaria-carrying mosquitoes ran rampant among the citizenry. Our town had enveloped itself in a Dickensian industrial haze. Sooty black coal dust rose into the air and descended again to cover sidewalks, gardens, rooftops, lines of cleanly washed clothes, windowsills —and lungs. Soft (bituminous) coal, universally used for industrial and residential purposes, produced this polluted air, and smoke-reducing ordinances carried little clout. Smells from the stockyards infiltrated the homes in the lower west side, and the waters of the canal were never refreshing. During the summer months of the late nineteenth century, the hilltops were as much as 15 degrees cooler.

When they relocated, the Longworths, Tafts, and Prices spoke of purer, fresher, healthier air; beautiful views; better water; and the abundance of other natural resources. No one could function properly without health, they said, and rightly so. As the flight to the hills became a financial possibility for the working classes, real estate hawkers pointed to the "better air" and "healthier climate" as prime selling points for building and buying homes. Early suburbs such as Mount Lookout and Fairmount were named for their scenic thrills, but other hills were christened Mount Airy and Mount Healthy.

One Cincinnatian would take the cause of the "Western Hills Beautiful" a step further. No local public relations braggadocio at that time compared with that of Cincinnati attorney, later judge, Hiram Rulison. He described the "mountainous" Elberon Country Club grounds, which he had purchased and planned to develop, in terms loftier than the Inspiration Point observation tower he erected on Overlook Avenue's peak—930 feet above sea level. In "Beauty Spots," Rulison's 11-page promotional booklet (price, one silver dime) published in 1912, he spoke of transforming the club into a modern suburb, "a hilly resort community . . . where the air is crisp and bracing; the sunshine tonic, and the green things, pleasant to the eye. In the springtime, the balmy breezes, nearly always from the West, are heavily laden with the fragrance of the blossom and the vine.

"People on the Western Hills sleep out of doors," Rulison went on to say, "because of the pure, bracing, health-giving, invigorating atmosphere. Here they recover and preserve their health without the expense of going to the higher and more lonesome altitudes in the far West. It is God's own country, on The Western Hills Beautiful, up where it's healthy."

In quite inspiring, if somewhat alliterative terms, Rulison climaxed his eloquence with a strong but subtle appeal to the pocketbook. "Health brings poise, peace, power, prosperity, plenty, pleasure, and all this spells success."

The Overlook Avenue subdivision was a resounding success. Rulison named the avenue parallel to Overlook between Cleves Warsaw Pike and Zula Avenues after himself. Residents no doubt continue to prosper, as they surely do on Prosperity Place.

MOUNT TUSCULUM

I THINK MY DAD worked on the Columbia Parkway steps, but I know he worked on the Ault Park job which included the [original] steps up to the bandstand. He was a good foreman; "Mr. Tom" was known real well by the biggest and the best in Cincinnati, like Byrnes & Conway, H. P. Kelly, and Frank Messer & Son. When he got hired for a job he went to the West End to hunt up laborers, white men and black men, workers who could stand the gaff [ordeal]. Working with cement then was a back-breaking job. No truck pulled up and poured the cement ready-made. It was made on the spot. Dad assigned each man a job and broke them in. There was the operator who determined how much water would be needed, how long to mix the concrete and so on. Water came from a fire hydrant, a water truck, or was carried by buckets from a pond. Sand and gravel were dumped on the site by trucks. Some men opened bags of concrete, one after another. It was all hauled by wheelbarrow to an enormous machine, a Koehring concrete mixer. Sand, gravel, concrete mix and water were put in one end and cement came out the chute at the other end. Wooden frames for the steps were built; workers with poles would smooth the cement out after it was shoveled in. Those workers were an independent bunch. You didn't pick up somebody else's shovel when you reported for work—each man had his own shovel. The day's work started early, and had to be organized.

Edgar George Maxwell,
lifelong resident of Columbia–Tusculum

Walk No. 21

2.8 miles

Columbia–Tusculum

WELCOME TO THE outgrowth of Cincinnati's first Hamilton County settlement, which was located a few miles east of this historic walk. Benjamin Stites, Reason Bailey, John Gano, and the other men and women who founded Columbia in 1788 are buried in the superbly maintained Pioneer Cemetery opposite the old Lunken Airport control tower on Wilmer Avenue. (Visitors are welcome; memorial plaque on site.) Although the steps in this walk are not actually legendary, the mighty expedition allows an intimate study of the communities of Columbia (Eastern Avenue and the "bottoms") and Tusculum (the "heights"). Other social landmarks are also highlighted, and Cincinnati's oldest homes, including glamorous clusters of rainbowed Victorians that may be compared favorably with those in San Francisco, are designated by pretty tile plaques. Also included is a generally unknown step-path through a stupendous bed of wild geraniums into Frederick Alms Park. From the park outlook, the settlement area, now abutted by the highly entertaining Lunken Airport, seems only a stone's throw away.

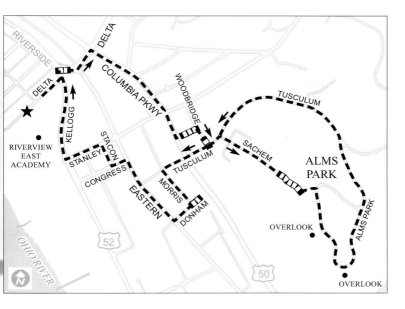

Near the Riverside Drive/Kellogg intersection, turn onto Delta Avenue alongside Riverview East Academy. Find a place to park on Delta Avenue or around the corner on Humbert Street.

- Walk north on Delta. Cross Kellogg at the light.
- Climb the one-flight **Delta Avenue Steps**, below the Pennsylvania Railroad overpass. Continue along the sidewalk under the railroad bridge to Eastern Avenue. This wide intersection once was crisscrossed by trolley tracks and later trellised by trolley-bus wires.
- Cross Eastern and continue up Delta.

    The Precinct restaurant is former Police Patrol House No. 6, which once housed a paddy wagon and horses (yes, another Sam Hannaford design).

    Yeatman Lodge No. 162 F. & A. M., across Columbia Parkway, is now the home of the Cincinnati Chapter of the Junior League.

- Right on Columbia Parkway; during the evening rush hour this stretch is not for the faint-hearted: fast vehicles on your left; faster (seasonal) lizards in the weeds to your right.
- Moving right along, you will observe (but do not take) single flights of **McDowell** and **Strafer Street Steps**. Cross Stanley Avenue; cross Columbia Parkway.
- Half a block along Columbia Parkway, watch for the first section of **Woodbridge Place Steps** on your left; one step down, lovely landscaped path, then up.
- Right at Woodbridge Place. Many decades ago, Johnny and Ruth Lyons set up housekeeping here; the marriage lasted but nine months; the divorce took nine years, or so say the neighbors.
- Up the remaining **Woodbridge Place Steps** at the cul-de-sac to Tusculum Avenue, where painted ladies beguile.

- Left; then right on Sachem Avenue.
- Continue your ascent of "Mount Tusculum."
- Once you reach the acme of Sachem you will spy the primitive **Alms Park Steps** leading into the woods; up you go.
- Into the clearing you will see, partially obstructed by a holly bush, a bronze likeness of Stephen Foster. He wrote many of his songs in Cincinnati, inspired by the Kentucky hills that his memorial faces.
- Turn right and follow the drive around to the Alms Park overlook, or climb the grassy knoll to take in the steps and view at the shelterhouse and the enlarged steps at the old stone slide.
- At the overlook, pause to observe Lunken Airport, originally designed to be Cincinnati's one-and-only. In the early spring, it is obvious why old-timers call it Sunken-Lunken, situated as it is between the Little Miami and Ohio Rivers. The Beechmont Levee and the dike (bicycle path) opposite now protect this energetic place—visited by Lucky Lindy in 1927. Check out the water tower marking the crest of Mount Washington.
- Continue down the drive, passing the Longworth wine cellar, the lower picnic area and medieval-style tower, back to Tusculum Avenue. Wide sidewalk on the left; down, down.
- Cross Columbia Parkway.
- Left on Morris Place. The fine entryway to the **Donham Avenue Steps** can be viewed next to Saint Stephen Church; taxpayers have inherited the otherwise going-nowhere stairs.
- Right on Eastern Avenue, passing through what was once the heart of the Tusculum business community. The Columbia Baptist Church boasts the oldest congregation in Hamilton County.

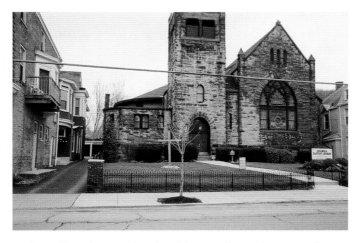

- Cross Tusculum to view the oldest continuously occupied home in Hamilton County at 3644 Eastern, built in 1804, just a few months after the Kemper Log House. Owned by James Morris (a.k.a. Morris Place), a tanner and manufacturer, the frame exterior covers an original log sub-structure.
- Before reaching Stanley Avenue, cross Eastern and cut through the railroad tunnel. Right on brick-lined Stacon Street to Stanley. Turn left on Stanley to Kellogg. Walk right (west) on Kellogg to Delta. Cross to the south side of Kellogg and take Delta to your parked car.

The Friendliest Hill

During the 1920s and 1930s, there were no happier residents in the East End than the children, rich and poor. The river, the hills, and the woods provided endless sources of fascination, sport, and adventure, during all seasons. In the winter, they skated on Wade's Pond, located on the Kellogg Pike. If the bottoms were flooded, there was ice skating all the way from Linwood to the East End, but this was a rare occurrence. They rode sleds down Carell Street, McCullough Street, and the best place of all—Tusculum Hill—starting at the top of the Alms Park hill, down Tusculum, over Columbia Road (which was just a gravel road then), all the way to Eastern Avenue. Adults threw cinders along the bottom of the hill so the kids wouldn't slide out into the Eastern Avenue traffic. Most used makeshift sleds. Older fellows had toboggans that held eight or nine people; they would take the little kids along, steering the sled with an ice skate. Considering how long was the hike back up Tusculum, four or five trips were about all anybody could endure. There was usually a fire at the top and one at the bottom to keep you warm. Some moms made extra mittens out of old long black stockings.

In the summer, Tusculum Hill was the scene of roller-skating. Girls and boys strapped the back of the metal skate around their ankle and clamped the front to their toes with a few twists of the skate key. God forbid you should clamp the skates on the wrong feet and have your legs spread out under you. If a friend didn't have a pair of skates, one skate each was good enough for both to scoot along. Other games were played: Go Sheepie Go, Boulder On Boulder Off (which predated Kick-the-Can), Hide-and-Seek, Swinging Statues, Foot Races, Marbles, and so on. Sitting on the porch swing was a game in itself, waiting for the summer hucksters: the hot tamale man, the umbrella man, the traveling salesmen that sold everything from socks to neckties, the man who took photographs of children on a pony. Wearing bib overalls and not much else, the boys waited to have their hair shaved off by Spicer, the traveling barber.

There was also time for skinny-dipping in the Ohio; not the Little Miami because it had leaches and step-offs, and there were rumors of quicksand. We also poked around in the dumps, particularly near the Charles Boldt Glass Works, where there were great places to hide in the wooden crates, and a kid could find a colossal colored-glass doorstop.

Shack-making was the *thing*. In the woods between Eastern and Columbia and around Alms Park there were as many as a dozen shacks. This called for membership: being sworn in, sworn to secrecy, and paying a nickel-a-week dues. Membership allowed you the privilege of building the shack; hunting up treasures to furnish it, such as chairs, table, lantern, etc.; or to gather wood or coal in the winter for a fire. An abandoned shanty boat down by the river made the best-looking shack, but tree shacks were the most fun to be in. Never a better night's sleep than in a tree shack on a balmy night. The most serious activity among the gangs was raiding some other gang's shack, taking all their furniture or kindling. One gang was called the Pike Apples, another the Carell Streetcars. One group collected World War I helmets, and their initiation was to have a bare electric wire touched to the helmet—it was a miracle that somebody wasn't killed!

After play, there was nothing better than a meal of scrambled eggs and brains from Findlay Market and going with dad to the saloon for a "growler" of beer—a round, tin pail with a handled lid, also used to collect blackberries from the woods in summer. Lazy days in an old johnboat, fishing for a supper catch—those days (according to Edgar George Maxwell) were the days when it was fun just livin'.

THE WESTERN
TERRACES

CINCINNATI'S HILLS, ALONG with the Ohio River, remain its topographical glory. I sometimes wonder whether native Cincinnatians sufficiently appreciate the beauty of the landscape around them, the difference it makes to have hills everywhere. . . . The stairs promote pedestrianism and provide the urban resident with a sense of intimacy with the environment. When we climb a stairs, we do not know what we shall find at the top.

John Clubbe,
Cincinnati Observed *(1992)*

Walk No. 22

3.1 miles

Riverside

THE RIVERSIDE COMMUNITY exists as a narrow band of cliff dwellers residing on two to three ridges between the Ohio River and Delhi Township, from Sedamsville to, and including, the Anderson Ferry landing. Some areas welcome transients, but for the most part Riverside is a close-knit community of working-class families whose roots go back for generations. In addition to the distinction of being Pete Rose's hometown, Riverside is also home of Clyde Street, the Number One Most Perpendicular Street in Cincinnati—with steps. The appealing and many Riverside steps complement the steep cross streets that extend from River Road—known as Slaughter Avenue—to the narrow, curvy, landslide-prone Hillside Avenue. Entering the Riverside community from downtown, old Hillside Avenue is obvious as the straightaway when River Road declines toward the river about half a mile from the old Penn-Central railroad station. About a mile further west is the one-way turnoff for this destination; if you miss it, turn right at Tyler Avenue. (The Anderson Ferry is about one mile west.)

Park along this residential stretch of River Road, separated from the main drag by a grassy park-like strip and a brown Riverside Community sign.

- Walk about one block west to ascend the rustic **Bowditch Street Steps.**

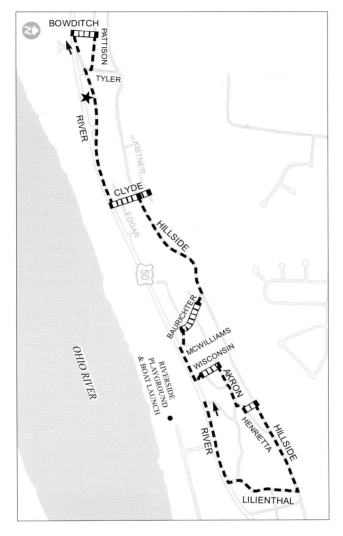

- Right on Pattison Street.
- Right on Tyler Avenue back to River Road.
- Left on River Road for about three blocks, crossing McGinnis Avenue. (The **McGinnis Avenue Steps** are partially private.)
- Left on the first dashing flights of **Clyde Street Steps**, climbing the hillside to Edgar Street.
- TA-DA: Clyde Street! And the final flights of **Clyde Street Steps**. Four blocks in length, Clyde Street ascends at a 30% grade. (What this means is that for every 100 feet in length, the roadbed tilts 30 feet.) Step on it, from beginning to end at Kistner Street. Pause to enjoy the view. Descend to Hillside Avenue.
- Left on Hillside Avenue for three hair-raising blocks (no sidewalk, but little traffic).

- Right on Baurichter Street to the graceful, aesthetically pleasing **Baurichter Street Steps**, accommodating the homes along Baurichter Street. The riverside view from this locus is marred by the presence of oil refineries, but the air is usually clear and the attractive public park and boat ramp are tremendous assets to the community.
- Left on River Road.
- Left on Wisconsin Avenue.
- At the bend, the **Wisconsin Avenue Steps** take you to Akron Avenue; turn right.
- At the hilly juncture of Akron, Henrietta, and Leland Avenues, you can't help but notice the wrought-iron fenced ruins of the original Riverside-Harrison school with gateposts worthy of rubbing.

- Continue northeast on Henrietta Avenue to the Henrietta Avenue Steps, just beyond the white church on the left. At the top of these steps, turn right on Hillside for one long block.
- Right on Lilienthal Street to River Road. If you are up for the challenge, cross River Road for an old-fashioned glimpse of the Ohio River and the Kentucky shore.
- Take River Road west to your parked car.

The Anderson Ferry

Native Americans and early settlers of the Midwest agreed on one point: the Ohio River was too wide to jump and too deep to wade. Making use of the Native American trails throughout southern Ohio and northern Kentucky, white settlers learned of the shallowest, most navigable river crossings because Native Americans often kept canoes in these locations. Along the Kentucky shore where Dry Run, later known as Dry Creek, met the Ohio River marked one of these shallow places; later on the creek would become the dividing line between Boone and Kenton Counties in the Kentucky Commonwealth. The location was perfect for a hand-oared, "fair weather" ferry service, and in 1807, the Boone County court established the toll at nine pence for a "man or horse" crossing.

In 1817, the ferry was privatized. George Anderson, a Boone County settler active in roads development, purchased a little more than 100 acres of riverfront east of Dry Run plus the ferry boat for $351.87. He built a stone home near the ferry lot and in 1832 was issued a permit to operate a tavern there. Various members of the Anderson family kept the toll-ferry service afloat until the Civil War. During that tumultuous period, the business changed hands several times, eventually ending up as the property of the Charles Kottmyer family when the war ended.

Kottmyer's first flatboat was constructed of wood, with a horse working a treadmill on either side to turn the paddle wheels. A bell announced departures. This craft was named Boone Number 1, after frontiersman Daniel Boone. In 1867, Kottmyer upgraded to steam. The hull was still wood, however, and a new craft was required every few years; thus came Numbers 2, 3, 4, 5, and 6, which were built by Charles's son Henry.

In the meantime, on the State of Ohio shore, the growing community had become known as Anderson Ferry Township until it was annexed to Cincinnati as Riverside. The road opposite the ferry was—and still is—called Anderson Ferry Road.

Built in 1937 by Henry Kottmyer, the side-wheeler Boone Number 7 is still in service today. It sports an all-steel hull and was converted to diesel in 1947. The Kottmyer family operated the ferry service for more than 120 years, but they developed financial interests elsewhere and the enterprise was put up for sale. In May 1986, Paul and Deborah Anderson bought this oldest continually operating Boone County business, and the Anderson Ferry was once again in the hands of the Boone County, Kentucky, Anderson family.

There are three boats currently in use at the Anderson Ferry. Boone Number 7 carries pedestrians, animals, and eight vehicles; Boone Number 8 is a flat barge pushed by tugboat "Little Boone" and carries 10 cars; and Boone Number 9, the lengthiest ferry, holds 18 cars. There are two other ferries crossing the mighty Ohio, at Augusta and Paducah, Kentucky; however, the Anderson Ferry is the only one privately owned.

Stories of the Anderson Ferry and its ongoing challenges through floods, gales, droughts, and the loathsome flotsam and jetsam are many. Early on, retrieving wandering livestock and stray boats set adrift by dangerous waters was a top priority for ferry operators. It was also a profitable venture, because owners were willing to pay a modest fee for the rescue. During the colorful 1990 autumn, Charles Kurault spent three days filming a segment about this transport for his television show *On the Road,* but it wasn't shown because of the approaching Gulf War.

Stories about the most prestigious person to ride the ferry are, however, easily obtained: Cincinnati Reds all-star Pete Rose lived on Braddock in Riverside, just a stone's throw from the ferry, where he collected tolls during his high school years. Family members are among those who still take the five-minute cruise on Saturdays and Sundays, when the wait is minimal. The Anderson Ferry departs about every 15 minutes from sunup to sundown. The whistle blows in the fog and during the peak-use summer months.

TWELVE

MEMORABLE

STEPWAYS

Walk No. 23

2.5 miles

Avondale

THE MEMORABLE STEPWAYS of this magical walk complement an area once referred to as Rose Hill, a name still apparent on buildings and street signs. Millionaires built the modest castles and mansions on Rose Hill around the turn of the twentieth century; the neighborhood is still exclusive and beautiful in its architectural detail. Get set for a treat.

Turn onto Winding Way Avenue from Dana Avenue and park.
- Proceed up Winding Way into the neighborhood of castles.
- Right on Redway Avenue. Left on Lenox Place.
- Right on Reading (rhymes with wedding) Road.
- Two major landmarks glamorize either side of Reading Road in the 3800 block.

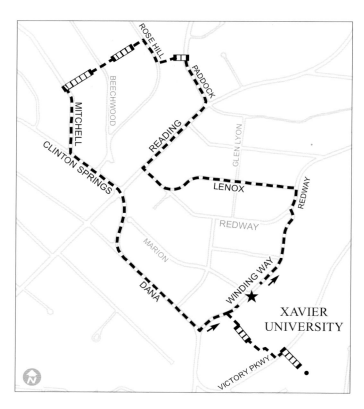

3863 is a three-story Indiana limestone castle that is now protected, and obscured, by a church wall; the castle was once owned by the Barney Kroger family. It is said that one of the main reasons the grocery magnate's stores were more successful than his rivals' was because Barney put price tags on the merchandise and other grocers did not.

3886, once owned by the Frank Herschede family, is an uncut-stone mansion behind a six-foot iron fence. Herschede became famous for the manufacture of hall and mantle clocks; they now specialize in designer jewelry.

- Cross Reading to Paddock Road.
- Descend Paddock about two blocks. Cross to the first set of **Rose Hill Lane Steps**, which are not easy to see; if you hit Stratford Avenue you have gone too far.
- This is a lovely three-block step-path. The first block brings you out to Rose Hill Avenue. Cross and go right about one-half block to Rose Hill Lane.
- Continue on Rose Hill Lane for two more blocks, crossing Beechwood Avenue to emerge at Mitchell Avenue.

- Left on Mitchell; left on Clinton Springs Avenue to walk along-side the grounds of the old Belvedere, once luxury resident apartments. Cross Reading Road and continue on Clinton Springs to Dana.
- Continue south on Dana Avenue to Winding Way.
- Left on Winding Way. At this point, you can continue to your parked car or go along to the south side of the Schmidt Memorial Fieldhouse, where an excellent stairway descends to the parking lot of the O'Connor Sports Center. Cross Victory Parkway and ascend the formal **Xavier University (XU) Steps** to go to the heart of the Xavier campus (private property).

The university boasts many beautiful staircases, old and new. The most up-to-date campus guide can be downloaded at www.xu.edu; clicking on Admissions sends you on a virtual tour of the buildings (stairs are not featured). Professors whose feet have trod the XU campus include Dr. Henry Heimlich, who has been credited with saving more lives than any other human being. On a completely different note, although it is now coed, women's feet were not allowed to trod the campus beyond the South Hall Theatre and Snack Bar at Dana Avenue and University Drive until the 1960s. Reputed to be haunted (by a woman?), the Jesuits razed South Hall in the 1970s.

Walk No. 24

2.8 miles

Old Clifton

PROOF THAT CLIFTON was founded as a patrician enclave rather than a working-class suburb is in its accessories. Gaslights on decorated iron poles date back to the 1840s. Add to these the decorative columns, seamed metal roofs, entry facades, wraparound verandas, weathervanes, gazebos, towers, gables, and outdoor urns that you may see on an afternoon or evening stroll, and you have a fine excuse to visit the otherwise minor steps located here. The reason there aren't many steps in Clifton is that founding fathers and mothers owned carriages.

Park in the upper parking lot off Clifftop Drive in Burnet Woods; this is the only place in Burnet Woods that you can park for two hours between 6 A.M. to 10 P.M. without a permit. During the University of Cincinnati school year, students and runners use the grounds; you may even see Tai Chi enthusiasts early in the morning, near the lake. (Be advised that the upper comfort station can be a rendezvous spot for fellows-of-the-afternoon.)

- Explore as many **Burnet Woods Steps** as you like, ending up at the lake. Continue along Burnet Woods Drive, with Martin Luther King Drive off straight ahead, until you spot the stone **Lakewood Avenue Steps** on your left.
- Follow the path up to the corner of Bishop Street and Lakewood Avenue; turn left.

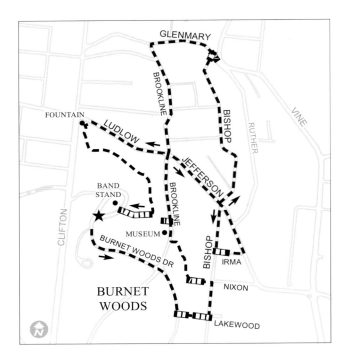

- Follow Bishop Street two blocks to Nixon Avenue. Go left onto the path that funnels into another set of **Burnet Woods Steps.** Take these back to the lake.
- Right on the blacktop path. (The once-public set of steps on the right before you cross to the museum now leads to private property; don't bother.)
- Cross Brookline Drive to the museum; if you desire, experience the steps leading to the picnic area or the double-dip slide, both built by the Works Projects Administration (WPA) in 1940.
- Follow Brookline out of the park to Jefferson Avenue. The chateauesque-style house at the southeast corner, designed by Samuel Hannaford and aptly named Parkview, was occupied by Cincinnati Mayor George "Boss" Cox from 1895 until 1912. Parkview is now owned by the Public Library of Cincinnati and Hamilton County.
- Right on Jefferson to Bishop Street; turn right. Continue two blocks to the stairway on the left: the **Irma Avenue Steps.**
- Take this little byway back to Jefferson Avenue.
- Left for about one-half block; cross Jefferson at Ruther Avenue.
- Right on Bishop Street to sample the pleasures of palatial living in Cincinnati in the mid-1800s.
- Follow Bishop Street to its end, about three blocks. The red brick streetcar barn here at the apex of Vine Street signaled the end of Clifton's exclusivity when the working classes

twelve memorable stepways

were finally able to get transportation into and out of the Basin.

- The steps at the bottom of Bishop are the **Bishop Street Steps**; the handful across Glenmary Avenue are the **Glenmary Avenue Steps**. Descend the **Bishop Street Steps**. Cautiously cross Glenmary.

- Left on Glenmary for one long block; left on Brookline Drive; right on Ludlow Avenue (Jefferson becomes Ludlow at Brookline).

- Cross Ludlow at Clifton Avenue, the oldest intersection in Clifton, to the path behind the fountain that leads into Burnet Woods. Follow the path through the trees. At the fork, go to the left, which brings you out to a picnic area just below the nature center. (Here is a cement slide, a favorite memory of mine [Connie J. Harrell]. As a child, my family often made day trips to Burnet Woods. Although we enjoyed the lake, the playground, and the nature center, most of all my brothers, sisters, and I enjoyed the cement slide. I think our parents liked it too because it wore out their children: Down the slide, then up the stairs, over and over again. We slept well on those nights.)

- Continue past the picnic shelter to the flagstone steps leading up to the bandstand and your parked car.

Walk No. 25

2.7 miles

Linwood

PARK ON EASTERN AVENUE near the Beechmont Viaduct.

- Climb the **Beechmont Viaduct Ramps and Steps** on the east
  side of the Beechmont Avenue Bridge. Explore the Beechmont Avenue Bridge. Sidewalks exist from one end to the
  other. The view from the levee bridge exposes the three distinct levels of Linwood. The first level is the bottoms, where
  many pert little homes amazingly continue to survive floodwaters and where in the 1950s there existed an official drag
  strip that paralleled the levee. The Eastern Avenue business
  and residential section is the second level. The high level of

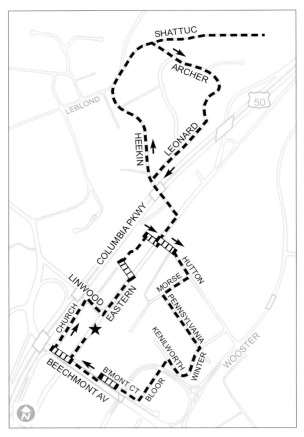

the community is perched up off Heekin Avenue, bordering
Mount Lookout. One of the city's oldest suburbs, annexed
in 1896, residents once considered Linwood to be "its own
little town."

- The Beechmont Viaduct was constructed in 1931 to prevent
  Mount Washington and Clermont County from being cut
  off by floodwaters of the Little Miami and Ohio Rivers.
  Farmers there provided much of the meat, grains, and produce that kept the city alive. Throughout the years, the levee
  has been reinforced to protect Lunken Airport and has been
  built up inch by inch to its present height.

- Proceed to the right on Beechmont Avenue. Turn right onto
  Church Street, right on Linwood Avenue, then left on Eastern Avenue. Walk past the Linwood Church to the **Ascen-
  sion Walk Steps**. These steps are well hidden just east of the
  home at 4826 Eastern Avenue. Climb to the top, and then
  follow the walk east into the adjacent elementary school
  grounds (formerly Linwood Elementary School), walking
  down the stairs in the front of the school to Eastern Avenue.

- Continue east on Eastern Avenue about three blocks. Turn left
  to climb Heeken Avenue, to explore the highest level of
  Linwood—a community with a definite southern ambiance.
  Turn right onto Shattuc Avenue, and follow it to its dead
  end. Here is Crusade Castle, a large two-story stone house
  with an interesting history, perched on a hilltop with a magnificent view of the Little Miami Valley. Crusade Castle has
  housed three groups during its more than 150 years. From
  1852 to 1917, the castle was the private home of the Jacob
  Feck family and the site of the Feck Winery, Vineyard, and
  Ice House. It served as the home of the American Academy
  of Christian Democracy from 1919 to 1922, and the headquarters of the Catholic Students' Mission Crusade from
  1923 to 1978. In the twenty-first century, it seems likely it will
  fall into the hands of upscale home developers.

- Return back on Shattuc, turning left on Archer Avenue to descend the hill, and right on Leonard Avenue back to Heeken. Turn left on Heeken and right onto Eastern Avenue.
- Follow Eastern back to the steps in front of the old Linwood Elementary School.
- Cross Eastern Avenue at the crosswalk, leading directly to the **Hutton Street Steps** and bridge over the former Little Miami Valley (Pennsylvania RR) tracks. These restored stairways were built in the 1930s by the Works Projects Administration (WPA) in a design similar to many other public stairs in Cincinnati. The steps lead to a quaint neighborhood nestled between several major highways with limited access. The streets within are so intertwined, seeming like a maze until you distinguish between the Circles and Courts.
- At the bottom of the steps, follow Hutton Street to Morse Street and go right.
- Turn left onto Pennsylvania Avenue; go about two blocks, then right on Winter Street. At the end of Winter Street, go right on Kenilworth Place (above, you can see Beechmont Avenue). Cross Kenilworth, then go left onto the Bloor Avenue pathway.
- Cross Beechmont Circle and continue on Bloor one block.
- Turn right on Beechmont Court, then cross Beechmont Circle again.
- Ahead are the **Beechmont Avenue Ramps and Steps**. Ascend these to the Beechmont Avenue sidewalk. Follow the sidewalk north, crossing the railroad tracks, and descend the steps on the other side to Eastern Avenue and your parked car.

Walk No. 26

3.7 miles

Chris O'Malley's Ridge Walk

THIS WALK, PERHAPS more appropriately a hike, links 12 stair-cases appearing in other walks, demonstrating just how far you can go in a vertical and horizontal fashion in this city of steps. The close proximity of these stairways allows for an extended hike up and down hills and steps and along many interesting streets that comprise a ridge overlooking downtown Cincinnati. The hike passes through beautiful, thriving neighborhoods as well as some urban blight, but having the experience of connecting the ridge views in one morning or afternoon is well worth it.

Starting in Mount Adams and ending in Fairview, the trip can be done as a round trip by doubling back, or the hike can be made with a friend and by bringing two cars, parking one at Fairview Park and driving the other to Mount Adams near the Art Museum.

- Descend the **Elsinore Avenue Steps.**
- Cross Gilbert Avenue and I-71 via Elsinore.
- Left on the west side of Reading Road to ascend the **Liberty Hill Steps (City View Steps).**
- Proceed west on Liberty Hill for about 50 yards, to ascend the **Hiram Street Steps** to Corporation Alley.
- Left on Corporation Alley; right on the **Young Street Steps.**
- Go left on Milton. After a short distance, you will see a walk through the Milton Street Park ascending to Boal Street. Either take the park walk, or continue past the park a short distance to ascend the **Broadway Street Steps** to Boal Street.
- Turn left on Boal Street, then right on Sycamore Street for one block.
- Left onto Mulberry Street.
- Take Mulberry Street to Main Street and ascend the **Main Street Steps** all the way to Jackson Hill Park, at the top. Enjoy the view.
- Pass Jackson Hill Park to continue one block on Eleanor Place. Look for the **Gage Street Steps** across from the stone building at 2206 Eleanor, The Malvern Place Apartments. Descend to Rice Street, going left on Rice. Right on Mulberry Street.
- Continue on Mulberry Street to Vine Street.

- Right on Vine for about one-half block to ascend the **Vine Street Steps** to Van Lear Alley.
- Continue climbing the **Ohio Avenue Steps** to Bellevue Park, and take in the view.
- Exit the park by turning left on Ohio Street; turn left on Parker.
- Left on West Clifton Avenue.
- Right on pretty little Klotter Avenue. Until 1996, there were public steps at the cul-de-sac of Klotter Avenue but, alas, no more. Turn right on Stratford Avenue.
- Left on Emming, where the superior **City View Place Steps** take you down to Ravine Street.
- Right on Ravine Street. Walk up the hill, then turn left into Fairview Park.
- As you follow the park road, take time to enjoy the terrific views of the city. Continue through the park to the **Warner Street**

Steps on the left side of the road.

- Descend the long and well-maintained **Warner Street Steps** to McMicken Street below.
- To return to your car, cross McMicken and look for the Metro bus stop sign. Board the Route 64 heading inbound towards downtown. (Ask for a transfer.) Exit at 7th & Sycamore to board the Route 11 heading out of town. Exit on Gilbert Avenue at Elsinore Avenue in front of television station WCPO, channel 9. Ascend the **Elsinore Avenue Steps** to your parked car.

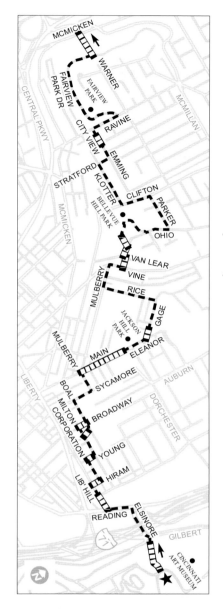

Walk No. 27

1+ miles

Old Milford

PARK ALONG MAIN STREET (U.S. 50) within the Milford business district, or on an adjacent side street.

- The charming shoppes of the old Milford business district, located on U.S. 50 across the Little Miami River, are framed by numerous flights of steps along Mill, Garfield, Elm and Locust Streets. These steps direct you toward the delightful residential neighborhood of historic homes on aptly named Mill, Mound, Cleveland, Laurel, Oak, and Hickory Streets. Walking west on these streets will also take you close to the Little Miami River banks. The river is surrounded by laurel, oak, hickory, elm, locust, and sycamore trees.
- At the end of Sycamore Street, past the playground of Memorial Park, are picnic tables that overlook the river. The bank is too steep here to walk down to the river safely.
- At the corner of Cash and Locust Streets, there is an opening in the split-rail fence that leads to a dirt path to the river's edge.
- If you stroll down on Water Street, you will see the cluster of stone buildings that served as the town center and grist mill during the nineteenth century.
- Nowadays this riverside town center is somewhat less bustling, but interesting nonetheless. Note the dandy little "shotgun"

twelve memorable stepways

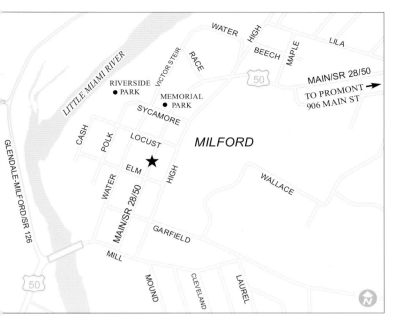

houses on the right side of Cash Street, so named by real estate agents because if you opened the front and back doors
you could fire a shotgun straight through the house.

- Main Street and its upper story High Street will take you on a
  satisfying tour of the more recent businesses in old Milford;
  you might want to pause in
  Memorial Park where the
  twin magnolias are magnificent in late April.

- Visit Promont House, the
  Milford Historical Society's
  lovely hilltop mansion,
  located at 906 Main Street
  (on Ohio 28 about three-
  quarters of a mile north
  of the junction of Ohio 28
  and U.S. 50); it is open
  on weekends.

Walk No. 28

5.1 miles

Norwood

EXISTING AS A three-mile-square island city within Cincinnati, this community's steps are particularly fascinating because they take us from an ancient Native American mound to commercial development, with pretty neighborhoods all around. Although the steps and paths are not in prime condition, and neither is the mound, the walk is an adventure. A handful of nice Norwood parks are seen; so too is the Park Avenue boulevard abutting the sprawling United States Playing Card Company.

Park on Smith Road just off Williams Avenue at I-71 (near the Rookwood Plaza).

- Descend the **Beech Street Steps**, located where Beech Street dead-ends at the above intersection.
- Follow Beech east, then around the corner and northward for several blocks to the corner of Beech Street and Robertson Avenue. On the corner observe the yellow-brick building that was once home to United States Playing Card Company. Continue walking on Beech past all of the company's buildings to the end of the street. The clock tower is visible for miles around.
- Near the end of Beech, go left on Park Avenue, then right on Forest Avenue, and walk under its long viaduct sidewalk.
- At Harris Avenue, turn right and walk east to Waterworks Park. Located at this site in the early 1930s were the Works Projects Administration (WPA) camp buildings. In the late 1930s, during the 1937 flood of the Ohio River, Cincinnatians stood in line here to draw water from Norwood's artesian wells.
- Walk into the park and explore the area. There are steps at the south side of

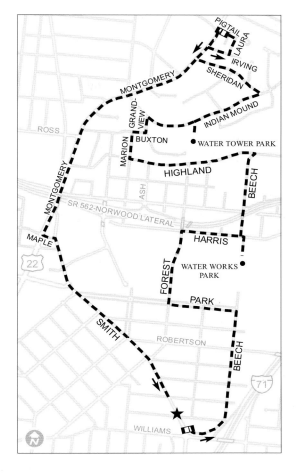

the park leading up to railroad tracks. At one time, people crossed the tracks here on foot to get to Beech and their jobs at United States Playing Card Company. Today, this pathway is closed. Retrace your steps back.

- Climb Beech Street, opposite, to exit the park. Finish Beech Street at Highland Avenue.
- Left on Highland Avenue, as you cross another active railroad track; go two Highland Avenue blocks.
- As you walk west on Highland, notice opposite Ash Street the remains of the **Ash Street Steps** which at one time ascended to Grandview Avenue and Water Tower Park. Continue on Highland, right on Marion Avenue, right on Buxton Avenue, left on Grandview, then right on Indian Mound Avenue to tiny Water Tower Park—elevation 790 feet and slipping.
- Walk into the park and follow the one-way loop around the neglected, painfully overshadowed mound to exit back onto Indian Mound Avenue, turn right, and walk east for two blocks.

- Left on Sheridan Drive. Right on Montgomery Road. Dominating the hillside across Montgomery Road is old Mount Saint Mary's Seminary of the West, now Our Lady of the Holy Spirit Center. After a previous engagement in Cold Spring, Kentucky, the Virgin Mary is said to be appearing in this location, perhaps taking advantage of the improved parking facilities.
- Right on Irving Place; left on Laura Lane.
- Left at the bend of Laura Lane to a blacktop path that crosses Pigtail Alley and introduces a cute little step-path.
- Descend the picturesque **Quatman Avenue Steps** from Pigtail Alley.
- Go left on Montgomery Road and walk south several blocks. After crossing the Ohio 562 expressway, turn left on Maple Street and walk to Smith Road. Turn right on Smith and walk south several blocks to your parked car.

twelve memorable stepways

Walk No. 29

1.8 miles

Oakley

THIS IS AN amiable and surprisingly satisfying tour of trim homes and lovely rock gardens. It begins at Oakley Park and continues through a wooded area containing oak trees for which the suburb is named and an exotic yellow poplar tree that flowers in late May (tulip trees, as they are also known, do not flower until they are 15 years old). The route transverses a small copse, winding up in Hyde Park Plaza.

Park in the Hyde Park Plaza parking lot, back by the little clock tower.

- Enter Oakley Park on the asphalt path to the left of the Oakley Community Center and Senior Center. Follow the path around to the second softball diamond. Do not take the first asphalt path you encounter; walk on to the second ball diamond. Here you will turn right onto another path that leads you down to the recreation center and the **Oakley Park Steps.**
- At the parking lot, follow the sidewalk towards the tennis courts and another set of park steps that lead behind the tennis courts.

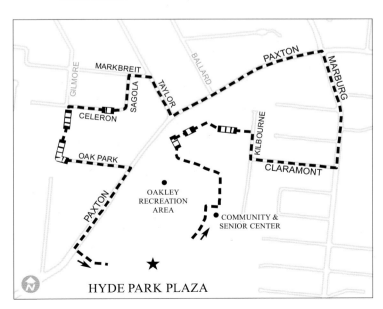

- Continue on past the tennis courts, veering right. At the cross-roads of two paths, continue straight ahead to the **Kilbourne Avenue Steps** and path. Ascend these to Kilbourne Avenue.
- Right on Kilbourne Avenue.
- Left on Claramont Avenue.
- Left on Marburg Avenue for two long blocks.
- Cross Paxton Avenue at the light; turn left.
- Cross Ballard Avenue; right on Taylor Avenue.
- Up to Markbreit Avenue; turn left.
- Left on Sagola Place. Follow Sagola around as it becomes Celeron Avenue.
- Ascend the **Celeron Avenue Steps**.
- Continue on Celeron to Gilmore Avenue.
- Look for a path across the street from Gilmore Avenue. This path is slightly hidden between two homes.
- Follow the fairly steep path that leads to the **Gilmore Avenue Steps**; descend.
- Follow the blacktop path and steps along the small copse.
- Left on the **Oakpark Place Steps** that are accented by a gaslight.
- Follow Oakpark to Paxton; turn right.
- Travel the distance to the stoplighted crosswalk leading into the main entrance of Hyde Park Plaza and back to your parked car.

twelve memorable stepways

Walk No. 30

4.2 miles

Crossing the Ohio River Bridges

SIX BRIDGES SPAN the river in these downtown areas; two are crossed in this walk. From east to west, the six bridges are:

- The **Daniel Carter Beard Bridge** (the **Big Mac Bridge**) carries I-471 across the Ohio River (vehicles only).

- The **Louisville & Nashville (L&N) Railroad Bridge**, now called the **Purple People Bridge**, was built in 1896 by the railroad. It is now restricted to pedestrians only, and painted purple.

- The **Taylor-Southgate Bridge** is the newest, completed in 1995, for both vehicles and pedestrians. It replaced an 1891 predecessor that was removed in 1992. Painted white, it has the most inviting sidewalks and steps of any of the six bridges.

- The **John A. Roebling Suspension Bridge** completed in 1866, was the prototype for John Roebling's Brooklyn Bridge. It was the first suspension bridge ever built, and engineers from around the world visit it. The bridge is used by both light vehicles and pedestrians.

- The **Clay Wade Bailey Bridge** carries CSX trains, vehicles, and pedestrians. It connects U.S. 25, U.S. 127, and U.S. 42 between Ohio and Kentucky.

- The **Brent Spence Bridge**, a double-decker, completed in 1963, carries the most vehicular traffic of any and connects I-75 between Ohio and Kentucky. It is becoming worn out, and slated for replacement in the next decade. It is restricted to vehicular traffic only, no pedestrians.

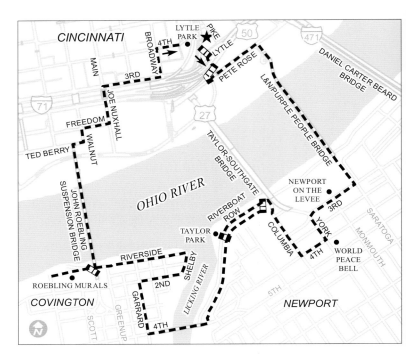

Park near Lytle Park on 4th, Pike, or Lytle Streets. Your walk begins at Lytle and 3rd.

- Descend steps to a walkway that takes you through a tunnel; go right to descend the steps to Pete Rose Way. Cross Pete Rose Way and go left (east) towards the pedestrian-only **Purple People (L&N) Bridge.**
- Cross the Ohio River on the **Purple People Bridge.** On the south side of the bridge is Newport, Kentucky. The large four-story building at the end of the bridge is Newport on the Levee, a center of retail shops, restaurants, movies, clubs, and game rooms. This building connects to the Newport Aquarium.

- Walk right (west) on 3rd. You might see the amphibious DUCK vehicle, which can be boarded for a ride on the Ohio River. Across 3rd Street is the Thompson House, an old mansion (now concert venue) that was the home of the inventor of the Thompson submachine (tommy) gun.
- Continue on 3rd, left on York Street, right on 4th Street. At the corner of York and 4th, you can observe the Millennium Monument World Peace Bell. The World Peace Bell is a replica of the Liberty Bell.
- Continue on 4th, right on Columbia Avenue to Riverboat Row. Note the stairs that climb up to the **Taylor Southgate Bridge**. For the present walk, we will not take these, but rather cross another bridge farther west.
- At Riverboat Row, either climb the steps to the path on top of the levee (below is a driveway along the river, part of Newport's Riverboat Row); or, should you choose to walk on Riverboat Row, you can climb another set of steps to the top of the levee farther west. The walk along the river will take you to Newport's Taylor Park, located east of the Licking River at the confluence of the Licking and Ohio Rivers. Follow the Taylor Park sidewalk and steps to 4th Street and the **Veterans Memorial Bridge**.
- Cross the **Veterans Memorial Bridge**. The Licking River is the boundary between Newport and Covington. You are now in Covington.
- Continue on 4th to the next stoplight. Walk right on Garrard, right on 2nd, left on Shelby, left on Riverside Drive. Take in the statues and historical plaques of some famous Kentuckians.
- Continue to the end of Riverside Drive onto the brick-paved pathway. Walk under the **Roebling Suspension Bridge** to view the Roebling Murals at the Covington Riverfront by artist Robert Dafford. Each mural depicts an important

event in the history of Covington; spend a few minutes
viewing all 18.

- Walk back to the steps leading you up to the **Roebling Suspension Bridge**. Cross the Ohio River on the bridge. Once on
the Ohio side, go right and continue along the sidewalk to
Freedom Way. Right on Freedom Way; left on Main Street
(Joe Nuxhall Way); walk over the expressway. Go right on
3rd, left on Broadway, right on 4th to your parked car.

Each bridge has its own personality. Each holds its own memories
in the lives of Greater Cincinnatians, because many families' roots
also span the Ohio River. A couple of "memories" you might not
learn about elsewhere: Cincinnati did not initiate the Suspension
Bridge project; Covington did. Cincinnati leaders opposed the idea
of a bridge, believing the piers would negatively affect the currents
and result in worse floods on the Ohio side and hazardous landings

for boats. Political pressure grew, however, and when Cincinnati leaders finally capitulated in 1849, it was with limitations they hoped would stop the construction. "The Cincinnati terminus . . . could not be the continuation of any Cincinnati street," the councilmen said, even though Covington and Cincinnati streets were perfectly aligned. Roebling put it between Vine and Walnut on the Cincinnati side. There it stands today, humming for more than 100 years.

In honor of Daniel Carter Beard, the man who started the Boy Scouts of America and wrote and illustrated *The American Boy's Handy Book* (1882), Boy Scouts may earn one of two badges crossing the Ohio River on bridges via special Boy Scout river walks. Completing one, the Dan Beard Five-Mile Riverwalk Trail, qualifies a Tenderfoot Scout of one of his second-class requirements. The 10-mile version of the river walk qualifies as a hike for the hiking merit badge. For information on these walks, go to www.danbeard .org/attachments/article/120/Riverwalk%205%20Mile%20 Trailguide.pdf.

It is not generally acknowledged that Beard's sisters were equally talented. *The American Girl's Handy Book* (1887), written and illustrated by Lina and Adelia Beard, was meant to perfectly complement, but not imitate, its twin. Together, the two books give a balanced perspective on youthful and energetic Ohio River living during that period. Lina went on to be one of the founders of a core group within the Girl Pioneers of America, an organization later absorbed into the Girls Scouts of America.

Walk No. 31

3.2 miles

Riverside Drive

JUST AS THE 25 sets of steps off the north side of Columbia Parkway were installed for commuters using the Little Miami commuter railroad, so too were steps installed along the north side of Riverside Drive. When the boatbuilding towns of Fulton and Pendleton existed where the lengthy strip called East End now stands—centered somewhat at Saint Rose Church and the Cincinnati Water Works—hundreds, perhaps thousands, of frame homes sat perched on the hillsides that would eventually be leveled for Columbia Parkway and the Pennsylvania Railroad. Although these convenient stairways once laced together these energetic neighborhoods from Kemper Lane all the way to the Beechmont Levee, only those east of the Rookwood Railroad Crossing to Delta Avenue are still somewhat active. The railroad is also somewhat active, although it may be converted to a bicycle path in the near future. Cross your fingers.

Drive to Riverside Drive and Lumber Street, and turn on Lumber. Park your car behind Saint Rose Church.

- Look out upon the Ohio River. Turn around and take note of the floodwater gauge on the backside of the church. It marks the flood stages over the past 130 years. None has come close to the disastrous flood of 1937, thankfully, due to the installation of the Meldahl Dam upriver, and the Markland Dam downriver.
- As you leave the parking lot, look up to the clock tower. The spire has a clock on each of four sides so one would be visible to both passing cars on Riverside Drive and to passing boats on the Ohio River.
- Out on Riverside Drive, go right (east). Just past Gotham, cross to the north side of the street and ascend the **Gotham Street Steps** at 2618 Riverside Drive, a major bus

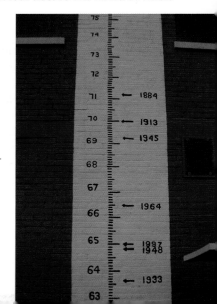

stop. Cross the railroad tracks to Hoff Street. Two sets of steps service the residents of Hoff Street. Turn right on Hoff and walk east to St. Andrews Street, crossing the tracks again to descend the steps back to Riverside Drive.

• Turn left (east) on Riverside Drive for several blocks. Enter the Wenner Street Underpass (built in 1917). On the other side of the tunnel, walk up to Walworth Street on steps bordered by a fancy railing and stone pillars. Go to the right (east) along Walworth Street. Many of these homes have a great view of the Ohio River.

• At the end of Walworth, cross Delta Avenue and Eastern Avenue, then proceed along the east side Delta sidewalk under the railroad viaduct. Descend the **Kellogg Avenue Steps** and cross Kellogg to the south side. On your left is the recently completed Riverview East Academy, uniquely built 17 feet above ground on stilts to prevent structural damage from floodwaters.

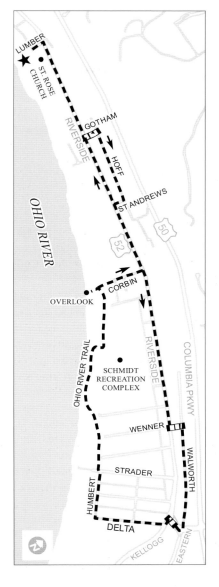

• Walk straight ahead on Delta Avenue to the park, then turn onto Humbert Street. Walk two blocks to the Ohio River Trail, accessible at Humbert and Stadtler.

• Follow the Ohio River Trail west for several blocks until it ends at Corbin Street near an overlook of the river. Along the way, enjoy an earlier overlook reached by walking across a grassy area to a low concrete wall. Take in the view of the Ohio River and northern Kentucky. Back on the Ohio River Trail, continue past the very colorful play area and the

baseball diamonds on your right to the Corbin overlook with stone pavers, benches and a flagpole. Notice the initials of the four compass points set in the stone pavement.

· Turn around and proceed north along Corbin to Riverside Drive. Turn left and walk west the few blocks back to your parked car at Saint Rose Church. It's not too far. You will see the clock tower.

twelve memorable stepways

Walk No. 32

3.7 miles

Sayler Park

SAYLER PARK, ORIGINALLY called Home City, represents the west-ernmost section of the John Cleves Symmes Purchase. It occupies a cozy niche a little over three miles west of the Anderson Ferry; those three curvy miles are full of river and river-related industries such as asphalt, gravel, sand, ice, and, of course, oil—traffic that shaped this community. The incidental steps here, mostly six to eight risers each, have sufficed as entryways from River Road public transportation for decades; they are memorable for their numbers and because they suggest such an awfully civilized touch. What makes this walk especially worthwhile is the genteel yet tough atmosphere of this "typical midwest American hometown," one that survived many floods, including the 1997 "Rivers Unleashed," and a devastating 1974 tornado. As a bonus, you get to visit Cincinnati's tiniest park. Plunked mid-intersection of River Road and Thornton Circle is the .01-acre Thornton Park, a sort of Native American reservation.

Enter Sayler Park from River Road via Gracely Drive (at the traffic light), and find a parking space on Gracely Drive (which runs parallel to River Road) somewhere between Zinn Place and Ivanhoe Avenue.

- Walk west on Gracely Drive to Monitor Avenue. As you pass
  Ivanhoe and Twain Avenues, you may want to walk the

short block to their end and view the steps accessing River Road. The section of River Road between Ivanhoe and Twain is inaccessible, due to accumulation of debris and overgrown vegetation, which at times completely blocks the sidewalk. U.S. 50 is a busy, high-speed highway and the sidewalk runs directly adjacent to the street without a protective grass buffer.

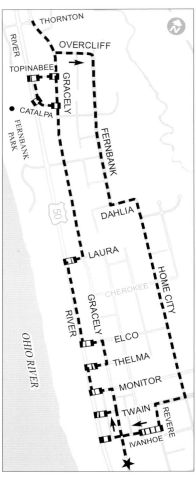

- Return to Gracely Drive and walk south on Monitor Avenue to the **Monitor Avenue Steps** leading to River Road.
- Turn right on River Road and proceed to the **Thelma Avenue Steps** to Thelma Avenue. Turn left on Gracely, and walk to Elco Avenue, following Elco to the **Elco Avenue Steps.** Turn right on River Road.
- Two blocks farther along River Road you're ready to ascend the **Laura Lane Steps.** Enter Laura Lane and proceed to Gracely. Take a rest in the small park on Laura.

twelve memorable stepways

- Cross Gracely Drive to the elevated sidewalk on the north side; left on Gracely for about six blocks. The nicely restored homes get pretty impressive here, and you will notice hand-railed **Gracely Drive Steps** accommodating them.
- Continue along Gracely or cross to Catalpa Avenue to test the **Catalpa Avenue Steps**, following the horseshoe-shaped street to the **Topinabee Drive Steps** and back to Gracely.
- Walk just a little further on Gracely to Thornton Park and statue. Take a gander at the steamboat gothic homes once owned by river captains.
- Begin your return along Gracely; go left on the Overcliff Avenue elevated sidewalk.
- As Overcliff becomes Fernbank Avenue, you head toward the Fernbank Golf Club. Once dotted by ancient Native American mounds, the only visible hump left is currently identified as Hole number 3, on your left.
- Left on Dahlia Lane.
- Right on Home City Avenue about three-quarters of a mile, passing Sayler Park School.
- Right on Twain Avenue.
- Left on Revere Avenue. About half a block down Revere you will see the lengthy portion of the **Ivanhoe Avenue Steps**, descending into a ravine and coming up the other side onto Parkland Avenue. Follow Ivanhoe to your parked car.

Walk No. 33

1.8 miles

University of Cincinnati

Steps galore decorate the many hillocks that make up the sprawling University of Cincinnati campuses, and plans are being considered to link the main and medical campuses to proposed rail transportation. In the meantime, this tour covers only the main campus and concentrates on areas with spectacular steps, some of them decades old. During your walk, you will see as many steps as you will climb—hundreds of them. Call the Office of Admissions ([513] 556–1100) for a copy of the official map and information on guided tours.

Park at a two-hour meter on Calhoun Street (one-way west) or McMillan Avenue (one-way east).

- On Calhoun Street, about one block east of Clifton Avenue, locate the YMCA. Descend the steps along the west side of the YMCA. At their bottom, continue straight ahead on Corbett Drive to its cul-de-sac.
- Move over to the sidewalk and continue north alongside the Patricia Corbett Theatre. Pass through the glass double doors of Memorial Hall to the College-Conservatory of Music (CCM) courtyard.
- Turn right on the courtyard road, CCM Boulevard, and follow it to Corry Street, which runs east parallel to Calhoun alongside the running track at Ben and Dee Gettler Stadium.

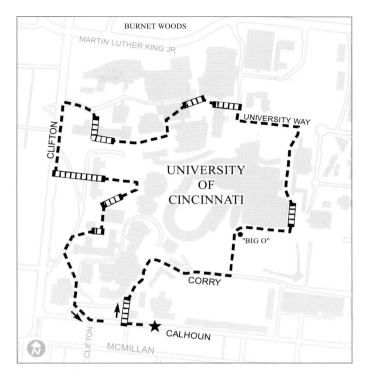

- Walk east on Corry. Across the street from the main entrance to Gettler Stadium, enter a wide walkway, O'Varsity Way, which goes north.
- Follow the wide, red-brick sidewalk north to the Myrl H. Shoemaker Center. Outside the Richard E. Lindner Athletics Center, located just west of the Fifth Third Arena at Shoemaker Center, stands a bronze statue of basketball star Oscar Robertson, the "Big O." View the plaque and statue donated by Robertson's friend and attorney, J. W. Brown.
- Go right past the "Big O" and continue along a sidewalk to the end of the Shoemaker Center and the backside of a very large black scoreboard.
- Once past the Center, turn left (north). Continue to walk past the ticket office and descend two flights of steps. This brings you to Armory Fieldhouse (red doors) on the left, and French Hall on the right. As you continue to walk, notice to your left the Sigma Sigma Commons amphitheater. Continue to walk north to a broad east–west sidewalk, University Way.
- Turn left and walk west on University Way. You will see the large Engineering Building, with several chimneys on its roof. Continue to the end of University Way at Main Street.
- Cross Main Street, and walk north (right) to a long, broad flight of steps at the north end of the Engineering Building.

- Ascend the many flights of steps between the Walter C. Langsam Library and the brand new Engineering Research Center, a world-acclaimed design by Michael Graves. Cross the spacious, nautilus-motif library square to ascend the sturdy maroon metal steps to the Zimmer Auditorium rooftop.
- Diagonally cross the rooftop; turn left. You are now entering the university's original quadrangle, with old Baldwin Hall as its centerpiece, Old Chemistry Building to the right, and Swift Hall to the left. Turn right to follow the sidewalk in front of the Chemistry Building.
- Continue through the quadrangle past Braunstein Hall, and descend steps at the west side of this building to Clifton Court. The building straight ahead is the Design, Architecture, Art, and Planning (DAAP) Building. Go left on Clifton Court to Clifton Avenue.

twelve memorable stepways

- Walk two blocks to ascend the well-laid, art deco handrailed **McMicken Hall Stairs**. The present McMicken Hall replaced the original McMicken Hall, the campus's first building, in 1950; many original red bricks were used in the construction.
- Walk through the breezeway in the center of McMicken Hall, crossing a slate floor, onto Commons Way. Make your way through the area known as McMicken Commons to Tangeman University Center (white doors and a clock tower). This facility houses the University of Cincinnati Bookstore as well as restaurants, refreshment stands, and restrooms—a great place to take a break.
- Back out on the Commons, proceed southwest towards the University Pavilion, the glass-paned building on your left. Ascend the steps to the front of the pavilion, walk to its northwest corner, and turn left (south) passing the delightful water sculpture on your right.
- Continue straight ahead towards Dyer Hall. Ascend the steps on the right and follow the walkway around Teachers College.
- Left on the Blegen Library walkway. Blegen Library, the most impressive old building on campus, has interesting architectural details inside and outside, including Rookwood fountains. Walk past the flattering statue of William Howard Taft up to Calhoun Street and your parked car.

Walk No. 34

2.8 (or 4.5) miles

Westwood

THIS CHEERY WALK takes you through an utterly charming community of well-maintained newer homes within an older suburb setting. Founded by the likes of James Gamble and Michael Werk, who built magnificent residences along what is now Werk Road, many smaller homes were once summer cottages of wealthy Cincinnatians. It is a tragedy that the Werk Castle, once decorating the corner of Werk Road and Harrison Avenue and modeled after a chateau in Blois, France, is no longer with us.

Werk was a vinter and silk-hat maker (neighbors raised silkworms to accommodate his trade), and, with Gamble, co-owner of the Cincinnati & Westwood Railroad. Gamble was so enamored of Westwood that he planted thousands of trees along his street and constructed the first cement sidewalk. He also gave carriage tours to promote development. The stairways of Westwood are neighborly and fun to discover.

Park at the southeast end of the Western Hills Plaza, near Glenway Avenue and Werk Road (there is a convenient entrance from Werk Road at this point).

- Cross at the light to hike down the left (east) side of Glenway Avenue for about three blocks. Across Glenway at Lumardo Avenue sits a yellow brick, tile-roofed building with stained glass windows and other architectural details worth investigating.

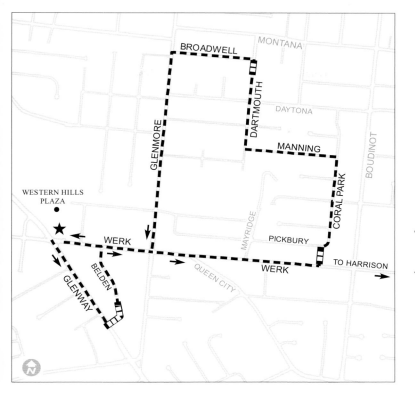

- Relatively opposite Our Lady of Lourdes School are the green-handrailed **Belden Circle Steps,** which probably were built for the convenience of the schoolchildren. This step-path leads to the center of Belden Circle.
- Follow Belden to its exit on Werk Road.
- Right on Werk Road. Cross Glenmore Avenue at the traffic light. Cross Werk.
- Continue along Werk Road, passing the spot where Queen City Avenue begins, crossing Mayridge Court, passing by a fine row of 1930s red-and-yellow-brick apartment buildings, watching for the **Pickbury Drive Steps** on your left (there is a Metro bus stop at the site).
- Left on the **Pickbury Drive Steps.** Right on Coral Park Drive about three blocks to Manning Avenue; turn left.
- Manning dead-ends into Dartmouth Drive, which is a bi-level street connected by steps.
- Right on Dartmouth three blocks, crossing Daytona Avenue, to the no-outlet end of Dartmouth.
- Ascend 17 tree-overhung **Dartmouth Drive Steps.** Descend nine more.
- Left on Broadwell Avenue.

- Left on Glenmore Avenue for about seven blocks. Turn right onto Werk Road and continue to Western Hills Plaza and your parked car.

Add historical interest to this walk by continuing on Werk Road to Harrison Avenue before you ascend the **Pickbury Drive Steps.** The glittering Tudor-style residence belonged to the Nipperts of University of Cincinnati stadium fame. Going left one block on Harrison, the three gorgeous homes you see were built between 1901 and 1903 by other Westwood pioneers. Left on McKinley to Werk. Back to Pickbury Drive. This is a 1.5-mile diversion.

twelve memorable stepways

bibliography

Books and Periodicals

Abbe, Truman. *Professor Abbe and the Isobars: The Story of Cleveland Abbe, America's First Weatherman*. New York: Vantage Press, 1955.

Bakalinsky, Adah. *Stairway Walks in San Francisco*. Berkeley: Wilderness Press, 1995.

Bakalinsky, Adah, and Larry Gordon. *Stairway Walks in Los Angeles*. Berkeley: Wilderness Press, 1995.

Beard, D. C. *The American Boy's Handy Book*. Rutland, Vt.: Charles E. Tuttle, 1973.

Beard, Lina, and Adelia B. Beard. *The American Girl's Handy Book*. Rutland, Vt.: Charles E. Tuttle, 1972.

Beaver, Joseph T. Jr. *I Want You to Know Wendell Phillips Dabney*. Mexico: Impresora Ancora, 1958.

Cauffield, Joyce V. B., and Carolyn E. Banfield, eds. *The River Book: Cincinnati and the Ohio*. Cincinnati: Program for Cincinnati, 1981.

Cincinnati: Days in History. A bicentennial almanac published by the Cincinnati Post, 1988.

Cincinnati Parks. Cincinnati Board of Park Commissioners, 1988. Updated edition of booklet published in 1953, written by John Travers Moore.

City Hillside Stair Study. City of Cincinnati: Office of Architecture and Urban Design, Division of Engineering, 1980. Compiled by Jim Mills.

Clubbe, John. *Cincinnati Observed: Architecture and History*. Columbus: Ohio State University Press, 1992.

Conrad, Mary T. "Remembering Caroline." *Journal of the Cincinnati Historical Society* 48 (1990): 17–20. Article about Caroline Williams.

Cronin, John F. "The Elsinore Tower." *Bulletin of the Historical and Philosophical Society of Ohio*, January (1951): 47–49.

Dabney, Wendell P. *Cincinnati's Colored Citizens: Historical, Sociological and Biographical*. Cincinnati: Dabney, 1926.

Dandridge, Raymond. *Penciled Poems*. Cincinnati: Powell & White, 1917.

Davis, R. A. "Land Fit for a Queen: The Geology of Cincinnati." In *The River Book: Cincinnati and the Ohio*, edited by Joyce V. B. Cauffield and Carolyn E. Banfield. Cincinnati: Program for Cincinnati, 1981.

Day, Doris. *Her Own Story*. New York: William Morrow, 1975.

Designation of 716 Mount Hope Avenue as an Historic Site. Materials presented to the Cincinnati City Council, 29 July 1994, by Leon A. Meyer, Director, City Planning Department, and the Price Hill Historical Society.

Dickens, Charles. *American Notes*. London: Chapman & Hall, 1842.

Dittly, Bernard. *Riverside Pride: A History of the Civic and Welfare Club*. Cincinnati: Neighborhood Studies Project of the Cincinnati Historical Society, 1982.

DuSablon, Mary Anna. *Who Killed Audrey Pugh?* Unpublished manuscript.

———. *Cincinnati Recipe Treasury: The Queen City's Culinary Heritage.* Athens: Ohio University Press, 1989.

Feck, Luke. *Yesterday's Cincinnati.* Cincinnati: Writer's Digest, 1975.

Guide to Art and Architecture in Cincinnati's Parks. Cincinnati Park Board, 1995.

Guiles, Fred Lawrence. *Tyrone Power: The Last Idol.* San Francisco: Mercury House, 1990.

Home Tour Committee. "Holiday Home Tour." *Price Hill Historical Society Bulletin,* January 1997.

Horning, Deborah. "Our Founding Fathers." *Price Hill Historical Society Bulletin,* October 1991.

Horning, Deborah, Rob Geiger, and Julie Hotchkiss. "Price Hill's Neff Mansion." *Price Hill Historical Society Bulletin,* 1996.

Inventory and Appraisal of Historic Sites, Buildings and Areas. Cincinnati: City Planning Commission, 1960.

Knoop, Mary Ann, Brenda Lugar, and Bonnie Schneider. *Columbia Tusculum 1788–1988.* Cincinnati: Columbia Tusculum Community Council, 1988.

Koehler, Lyle. *Westwood in Ohio: Community, Continuity, and Change.* Cincinnati: Westwood Civic Association, 1981.

Langsam, Walter Consuelo. *Profiles of America: Cincinnati in Color.* New York: Hastings House, 1978.

Madsen, Heather, Chris Neely, Keith Neumann, and Amy Pyle. "Index of the Work of Caroline Williams." *Journal of the Cincinnati Historical Society* 48 (1990): 72–75.

Moore, Valda. "Glenway-Elberon Heights." *Price Hill Historical Society Bulletin,* December 1996.

Morsbach, Mabel. *We Live in Cincinnati.* Cincinnati Lithographing, 1961.

Mount Auburn: Prospect Hill Historic Conservation Plan. Cincinnati Planning Commission, Office of Architecture and Urban Design, 1981.

Neff, Jack and Skip Tate. *The Insiders' Guide to Greater Cincinnati.* Lexington, Ky.: Lexington Herald-Leader; Manteo, N.C.: The Insiders' Guides, 1995.

Neighborhoods. Glendale, Ohio: Willow Press, 1989.

Over-the-Rhine: A Description and History. Cincinnati: Historic Conservation Office, 1995.

Peck, Herbert. *The Book of Rookwood Pottery.* Cincinnati Art Galleries, 1991.

Price Hill: Preserving Yesterday, Today, for Tomorrow. Cincinnati: Price Hill Historical Society, 1990.

Quinn, Ralph. *Price Hill: Cultural and Historical Points of Interest.* Price Hill Historical Society, n.d.

Redman-Rengstorf, Susan. "The Queen City Through the Eyes of Caroline Williams." *Journal of the Cincinnati Historical Society* 48 (1990): 3–16.

Rulison, Hiram M. *Beauty Spots: In and About Glenway-Elberon Heights.* Cincinnati, 1912.

Schweitzer, Father Al, and Henry Gerbus. *The History and the Story of Findlay Market and the Over the Rhine.* Cincinnati, 1980. Reprint of 1974 booklet.

Stowe, Lyman Beecher. *Saints, Sinners, and Beechers.* Indianapolis: Bobbs-Merrill, 1934.

WPA Guide to Cincinnati, The. Cincinnati Historical Society, 1987. Edited by Harry Graff. Reprint of Ohio Writers' Project, *Cincinnati: A Guide to the Queen City and Its Neighbors, 1788–1943.* Federal Writers' Project of the Works Projects Administration (WPA), Cincinnati, 1943.

Wagner, Richard M., and Roy J. Wright. *Cincinnati Streetcars: No. 2, The Inclines.* Cincinnati: Wagner Car Co., 1968.

———. *Cincinnati Streetcars: No. 8, Through the Thirties.* Cincinnati: Wagner Car Co., 1968.

Weybright, Victor. *Spangled Banner: The Story of Francis Scott Key.* New York: Farrar & Rinehart, 1935.

Williams, Caroline. *Cincinnati Scenes: Sketches by Caroline Williams.* Cincinnati: Landfall Press, 1973.

———. *Cincinnati Steeples, Streets and Steps.* Burlington, Ky.: Penandhoe Press, 1962.

Newspapers

Cincinnati Enquirer

Baden, Patricia Lopez. "I'll Huff, I'll Puff, I'll Get up Straight Street." 19 November 1990.

Delguzzi, Kristen. "Really Dig Snow? Try Straight Street." 9 January 1996.

"50 Years Ago in Cincinnati: January 24, 1886." 24 January 1936. Annie Oakley news.

Findsen, Owen. "There Freedom Rings: Greater Cincinnati Sites Mark a Path Through Area's Black History." 7 February 1997.

Findsen, Owen. "Slick Nick Longworth Left His Mark." 12 May 1996.

"Grandin Road Viaduct Over Delta Avenue." 19 April 1901.

Harbaum, Bob. "Update." 16 October 1980. Update on Bald Knob Mountain.

Howard, Allen. "Upland Seeking Place in the Sun." 24 July 1996, Metro section.

Hunter, David. "The City's Stairs." Photographs by Allan Kain. 22 June 1980, Magazine.

Keating, Michael E. "Straight Up Straight." 25 November 1991.

Lane, Peggy. "Overlooked Overlooks." 7 May 1988.

McWhirter, Cameron. "Pain Lovers Run Straight Up." 17 December 1995.

Miller, Mildred. "How Halt Howie?" 5 December 1952.

Moores, Lew. "Editor Remembered as 'Renaissance Man.'" 24 February 1991. Article about Wendell Dabney.

"Mt. Lookout Residents Throng Square to Take Part in Rededication Program." 24 October 1952.

"Pioneer Florist Dies." 16 February 1925. Dwight Herrick, partner of Jackson family, obituary.

Sands, Gilbert. "Howie Defends Traffic 'Hurdles.'" 6 December 1952.

Turmell, Mike. "Ravine Steeped in Memories." 10 June 1991.

Weintraub, Adam. "Ice Storms Given a New Slant." 11 February 1994. Article about Straight Street.

Cincinnati Times-Star

Brinkman, Walter. "Plans for Ault Park Pavilion and Tower Are Approved." 20 December 1927.

"Dabney." 5 June 1952. Wendell Dabney obituary.

"Founder of College of Music Dies After Brief Illness." 14 February 1912. Peter Rudolph Neff obituary.

"Iphigene Bettman: Hereabouts." 7 March 1951. Elmhurst viaduct changes to a footbridge.

Ludwig, Charles. "Schuetzenbuckel Memories Recalled by Picnickers of More Than 50 Years Ago." 6 February 1939.

Michelson, Herb. "Annie Oakley Got Her Start Here." 29 March 1958.

"Mt. Echo Park Will Rival Eden Park." 17 August 1912.

"Tribute Is Paid to Negro Editor on 84th Birthday." 4 November 1949. Article about Wendell Dabney.

"Wendell Dabney." 5 June 1952. Editorial.

"'Werk Castle,' Once Famous as Center of Brilliant Social Functions, Passes." 12 September 1935.

Cincinnati Post

Clopton, Bill. "Vandals Rain Missiles Down on Residents Living Below Overpass." 8 February 1958.

"Dancing Season Opens at Ault Park Center." 18 June 1962.

Hunter, Ginny. "Landslide City, U.S.A." 7 November 1981.

Mayo, Harry. "Schuetzenbuckel Gone but Fairmount Remembers." 11 November 1950.

"Neff Mansion Condemned After Section Collapses." 27 March 1944.

"Oakley Rites." 6 November 1926. Annie Oakley obituary.

Petrie, Laura. "Current SCPA Location Site of 1831 High School." 20 April 1996.

Segal, Eugene. "Worry, More Worry! What's the 'Whatzis' on Bald Knob?" 26 June 1933.

Wittow, Irv. "Annie Oakley: She Started Here." 20 November 1976.

Cincinnati Post & Times-Star

Steffens, Ray. "How Was It Named? Ravine Street." 19 September 1961.

Boone County Recorder

Fitzgerald, William. "One of Boone County's Oldest Business Institutions." 14 March 1968. Anderson Ferry documentation to 1865.

index

Page numbers in italics refer to photographs on those pages.

about the authors

Mary Anna DuSablon (1937–2005) walked the steps of Cincinnati and wrote about Cincinnati her entire life, promoting and celebrating the city's history and beauty.

The daughter of Bernadette Maxwell Martin and Cincinnati's Chief of Homicide Charles Edward Martin, Mary Anna was an active participant in the life of her city, serving as a Democratic Party election judge, directing drama at St. Xavier High School, and playing the organ at Saint Rose Church. She was employed by the Walnut Hills Branch of The Public Library of Cincinnati and Hamilton County.

In addition to *Walking the Steps of Cincinnati,* her publications include *America's Collectible Cookbooks: The History, the Politics, the Recipes* and *Cincinnati Recipe Treasury: The Queen City's Culinary Heritage.*

Connie Harrell (1952–) grew up in the Fairmount neighborhood of Cincinnati. She walked the hills of Fairmount to Roosevelt elementary school, to the neighborhood Shadwell Park and swimming pool, to local grocery stores, to the movies, to playmates' houses. After attending college and getting married, she moved away from Fairmount. Upon her discovery of *Walking the Steps of Cincinnati,* she began walking the tours of Fairmount, bringing back long forgotten childhood memories, making her very happy. Other walks led her to discover the beauties and charm of previously unexplored Cincinnati neighborhoods.

In 1973, **John Cicmanec** (1944–) came from Chicago to Cincinnati to attend graduate school at the University of Cincinnati. From there he found a career at the university, and made Cincinnati his home. In 2009, Connie told him about *Walking the Steps of Cincinnati,* and asked him to join her on the tours as some of the neighborhoods seemed somewhat forbidding for a single walker. Connie and he shared a love of history, of Cincinnati, and of walking. This book brought form to their endeavors.